ON WRITING SERIES

ALSO BY PETER M. BALL

ESSAY COLLECTIONS

You Don't Want To Be Published & Other Things Nobody Tells You When You First Start Writing

GENREPUNK NINJA ESSAYS

On Heinlein's Rules & The Rise Of The New Pulp Era

Here Be Dragons: Vanity Presses, Scams, And Publishing In The Digital Era

DANA VALKYRIE ADVENTURES

White Harbor War

SHORT STORY COLLECTIONS

The Birdcage Heart & Other Strange Tales

Not Quite The End Of the World Just Yet: Short Stories & Strange Futures

These Strange & Magic Things: Short Stories

What We Talk About When We Talk About Brains: The Red Rain Short Stories

Unfamiliar Shores: Stories

KEITH MURPHY URBAN FANTASY THRILLERS

Exile

Frost

Crusade

Unicorns, Fey, and a Hardboiled Dame: The Miriam Aster Duology

ON WRITING SERIES
SERIES POETICS & DIGITAL PUBLISHING

PETER M. BALL

GenrePunk Books (an imprint of Brain Jar Press)
PO Box 6687
Upper Mt Gravatt, QLD, 4122
Australia
GenrePunk Ninja Books: Genrepunk.Ninja
Brain Jar Press: www.BrainJarPress.com

Copyright © 2024 by Peter M. Ball. This book was originally submitted as part of a PhD thesis at the University of Queensland, 2024.

The moral right of Peter M. Ball to be identified as the author of this work has been asserted.

All rights reserved. No part of this book may be reproduced in any form or by any electronic or mechanical means, including information storage and retrieval systems, without written permission from the author, except for the use of brief quotations in a book review.

Cover design by Brain Jar Press

ISBN: 978-1-922479-96-9 (paperback) | 978-1-922479-97-6 (Ebook)

CONTENTS

Acknowledgments	vii
Towards A Nuanced Understanding Of Series Fiction *An Introduction*	1
Strange Liaisons *Understanding Series Verisimilitude And Serial Connections*	13
This Is Not An Ending *Series Temporality And Publishing Contexts*	38
Navigating The Ellipsis *Story, Character, And Endings In Series Works*	66
George RR Martin Is Not Your Bitch *A Conclusion*	91
Bibliography	103

ACKNOWLEDGMENTS

This book is an expression of my PhD research at the University of Queensland, undertaken during a particular challenging period which included the death of my father and a global pandemic. While it's true that no thesis—and no book—is completed without the support and assistance of others, this one owes considerable debts to those who supported me through this period.

In particular, I wish to express my gratitude to the University of Queensland and my supervisors, Kim Wilkins and Natalie Collie, for their advice and encouragement while writing the thesis from which this book emerged.

Writers rarely learn their craft in a vacuum, and this project has been informed by and supported by many people who asked questions, offered keen insights, and provided valuable discussion and ongoing support as my ideas developed. My thanks go out to Sarah Hobday, Margaret Ball, Sally Ball, Angela Slatter, Meg Vann, Kathleen Jennings, Joanne Anderton, Kate Cuthbert, Kate Eltham, Kevin Powe, Allan Carey, Nicola Logan, Nicholas Holland, and Adam Norris.

I dedicate this book to my father, Terry Ball, who would have been so pleased to see it finished.

TOWARDS A NUANCED UNDERSTANDING OF SERIES FICTION
AN INTRODUCTION

If the beating heart of the story lies not on the page, as Lisa Cron argues (69), but deep in the protagonist's past, then my own history may provide a useful starting point for understanding my fascination with series fiction. Just as characters are motivated by past experiences, acting on hurts and failures which occurred long before the first page, I am driven to my research by my own failings and dissatisfaction with authoring series works in the past.

I began my first series in 2009 when my novella, *Horn*, sold to a small Australian press who foresaw a strong market response. While accepting the work, the editor requested a sequel and I agreed with all the enthusiasm of an emerging writer eager to sign their next book. While I possessed no immediate plans or ideas for a sequel, the idea held some appeal. *Horn* owed a great debt to Raymond Chandler's *Philip Marlowe* stories, and some of my favourite moments in those tales were set up by their status as series work. I daydreamed of writing an endless number of books featuring the protagonist of *Horn*, Miriam Aster, and dove into the task.

Writing a sequel proved to be a terrifying experience, full of missteps and deadlines I struggled to meet. I produced a draft which felt too convoluted and separate from the first volume, setting it aside and writing a second story seeking a better fit. My writing instincts clashed with the task of writing a sequel and I second-guessed every creative choice. The events of the sequel felt beholden to the first book, yet unlikely to satisfy a reader who'd already experienced a completed character arc. Midway through the drafting process the first book, *Horn*, received nominations for best novel in two categories of the Aurealis Awards. I felt the weight of building expectations settle upon the sequel as *Horn's* success felt like a trick I'd pulled off by accident, then forced myself to clumsily reverse engineer.

Writing Bleed proved a frustrating experience, but it was completed and released in 2010 to a mixed reception. Intriguingly, a divide formed between those who read it as a stand-alone and those familiar with *Horn* before reading the second book. One reviewer, unfamiliar with *Horn* but aware of its existence, praised *Bleed* and suggested readers "be careful here Ball's series is habit forming and I'm already looking at getting my grubby mitts on Horn sooner rather than later" (*Bleed Review*). In contrast, a reviewer who had praised the first work felt the second work suffered: "what originally drew me to *Horn* was the freshness of it and how everything comes together. *Bleed*, for the most part, feels a bit derivative, and lacks the edginess of its predecessor" (Tan). This split intrigued me given my dissatisfaction with the creative process, as Tan's review echoed my own concerns around familiarity and expectations. Despite the publisher's interest in a third book, and perhaps a longer series, I focused my attention on other projects.

I've written other series works since then, seeking out opportunities to improve on my first experience. Each time, I expected the process to be easier and the question of reader expectations easier to navigate, and yet it remains an ongoing debate. Each new series work kicks off with a familiar debate: how much should the character change? Should I leave cliff-hangers and treat this like a serial, rather than a progression of stand-alone tales unified by an arc? How much knowledge of prior stories should I assume when drafting the newest tale? Despite multiple attempts, I did not find a satisfying answer, nor write a series that felt like I'd satisfied my ambitions and lingering distrust of the format.

When writing the *Dana Valkyrie* stories for this thesis, I have set out to answer the two questions that have plagued me since I first revisited a character and a setting: what is it that makes writing a series instalment different from writing a stand-alone work? How can an understanding of those differences lend themselves to producing stronger, more innovative series works?

The answers to these questions felt frustratingly difficult, as the poetic concerns of series fiction are oft ignored in both critical and commercial examinations of series and writing craft. My inability to find clarity around the expectations of a series speak directly to the challenge of writing them—as Mathew Salesses has noted, writing craft is deeply entwined with expectations (xv), and even oft-repeated advice such as the word "said" being invisible to readers is cultural, influenced by the tastes and expectations of a shared cultural background. In essence, "to learn craft is to learn how to use cultural expectations to your advantage" (4), and these expectations are never neutral. To learn the craft of writing of writing is to develop an awareness of the expectations brought to a text, which the writer can choose to conform to or reject. To be unable to predict what's expected from my series left me without a foundation for what might be considered "good" or "bad" writing.

While this book charts my research into these expectations, it also informed and was informed by my creative practice, charting elements which helped me develop my own framework for understanding what I expect from series as a reader and how I can frame those expectations in my own work.

It's notable how few resources there are articulating the expectations we have of series texts. As Shane Denson has observed, cultural studies of seriality have been "less interested in the seriality of popular forms than in the popularity of serial forms," with their focus on what audiences are doing with mass-produced serials rather than how they're created. This reluctance to tackle seriality continues through to the popular writing space, where advice aimed at the writer of series is often anecdotal or confined to surface level concerns

Despite the dearth of texts addressing the series on a formal or critical level, it's clear interest in writing series fiction is growing. At the beginning of my research in 2017, a Google search for writing a series brought up links to a series of blog posts. Three of the posts appearing on the first page of results focus on mistakes to avoid. One deals with math problems, one deals with plot structures, and the remaining four focus on practical tips for beginners based on the writers' own experiences. An Amazon.com search on the same topic brought up three texts of interest to an aspiring fiction writer, as opposed to writing for television: Karen S. Wiesner's *Writing the Fiction Series: A Complete Guide For Novels and Novellas*, Beth Daniels *The Beginner's Guide to Story Arcs for Trilogies and Series*, and Susan Palmquist's *Writing the Continuing Series and Trilogy*. Repeating this exercise in 2023, as I finalise my research, shows a rapid proliferation in both the quantity and focus of blog posts, and the number of writing guides overtly aimed at writers of series fiction have risen to nine.

Many of the popular writing texts available are focused on practical advice. However, even a cursory glance at the advice offered in these texts suggests that series fiction are not like stand-alone works, and they echo the dual expectations we have of series texts: each story must stand alone, yet be part of a larger whole. Yet the advice for dealing with this duality was frequently perfunctory, and rarely involved practical next steps. Similarly notable is just how new many of the texts were, and how quickly they proliferated. Both Daniels and Palmquist's books were less than twelve months old in 2017, and both were self-published. Six years later, the bulk of the books on sale are similarly new and published by the authors.

This same focus on reading experience is echoed in Joanna Penn's suggestion that "I think each book should be a stand-alone as well as being able to be read in sequence but it's hard to know what to repeat and also how to phrase it without sounding repetitious," (Penn), or when Karen Wiesner advises writers:

> *Each book in a series should come with your unbreakable promise to the reader that she'll get something extra, something more exciting and fulfilling, by following the series—something she wouldn't get with a book that simply stands alone (whether*

> as part of a series or not). Each book in a series must fulfil the handshake contract the writer has silently made with the reader: Stick with me, and I'll show you a world, characters, and adventures you'll never grow bored with (Introduction)

And yet, there were no effective tools that seemed to aid in the understanding of how series works differed from the stand-alone narrative. No advice to illuminate why the weight of expectations dragged against the second work. No structural guide that could adapt my understanding of narrative structure, setting, character, and the effective use of language through courses, workshops, study, and experience. For most writers, the production of a series remained a matter of intuition: they take what they know about writing a single narrative and extrapolate outwards into multiple instalments.

As a writer immersed in the logic of the publishing field, I felt these absences in our collective understanding. The logic of the field—or at least the parts I knew of and could access—concerned itself with the creative aspects of serial forms compared to the vast amount of awareness and information available for stand-alone novels, short stories, and other works. In both academic writing and commercially available tools aimed at aspiring authors, we have given series fiction little attention, suggesting its techniques and poetic toolkit closely aligned with producing stand-alone, self-contained narratives. My experiences suggested this was not true, and so I went in search of a means of explaining my discomfort. This thesis will seek to address why I struggled with the creation of series fiction by exploring the poetics of serialised stories, laying out how they generate effects that are distinct and separate from stand-alone narratives. However, in this chapter, I will argue that an awareness of series poetics already exists within the logic of the publishing field, although they are not understood as a unified and coherent way, and there are both critical and creative benefits to addressing the poetic devices of series fiction as a distinct subject from stand-alone narratives.

· · ·

I borrow the term "The Logic of the Field" from John B. Thompson and his study of the publishing field, *The Merchants of Culture* (11). Building on the work of French sociologist Pierre Bourdieu, Thompson employs the idea of the 'field' to understand the context in which agents within and around the publishing landscape assess decisions and take action (3-4). In doing so, he makes it possible to see that publishing is not one field, but many intersecting fields with their own distinctive characteristics, in which agents utilise particular forms of capital (5) and operate in relational ways, never existing in isolation (4). Most importantly, Thompson suggests that each field in publishing has its own distinctive dynamic, which he dubs the 'logic of the field,' or the conditions under which individuals and organisations active within publishing both 'play the game' and make decisions that allow them to 'win' by achieving creative and commercial goals (11). In doing so, Thompson neatly characterises and names the morass of informal and often practical knowledge that writers and other agents within publishing employ to navigate their careers. Indeed, many oft-quoted pieces of advice aimed at young writers—from "a writer must read" through to "know your genre" to "don't write to market" — genuflect towards the necessity of developing one's understanding of the logic of the field and the expectations of readers and other agents, even if they rarely articulate why and how these steps are useful in these terms.

Despite his terminology, Thompson does not suggest the intersecting fields of publishing are 'logical'. Rather, they represent the processes and preoccupations in play, and the context in which works are produced, distributed, sold, and consumed (294). In this respect, understanding the logic of the field makes it easier to identify why certain choices get made, even if they don't seem logical on the surface (295). While Thompson is focused on publishers, agents, and booksellers, writers on every level are active participants in the publishing landscape, and our work and careers are both shaped by the logic of the field and shape it in return.

Thompson's framing resonates because it reflects my own experience. As a writer, I have frequently responded to the logic of the field, making choices which reflect my growing understanding of the industry. Yet, I have not always been conscious of the logic underpinning those choices, even when they have been correct. Thompson offers the metaphor of grammar to understand this unconscious, experiential approach to navigating publishing. "Individuals know how to speak correctly, and in this sense they have a practical knowledge of the rules of grammar, but they may not be able to formulate these rules in an explicit fashion" (11-12). Agents within the field can play and win, even if they are unable to articulate why they've achieved success.

The metaphor of grammar serves two critical purposes here. First, it opens our understanding to way in which the Logic of the Field may be used intuitively, rather than consciously. Thompson makes this argument explicitly, when he suggests that the logic of the field may be understood in practical terms:

Individuals who are active in the field have some degree of practical knowledge of this logic: they know how to play the game, and they may have views about how the rules of the game are changing. They may not be able to explain the logic of the field in a neat and concise way, they cannot give you a simple formula that sums it all up, but they can tell in in great detail what it was like when they entered the field, what's like now, and how it's changed over time. (11)

I do not seek to discount this intuitive understanding of the field, particularly with regards to series fiction. Indeed, Thompson's framework makes it clear how many great series works can be produced without a formal approach to series poetics. While a writer must understand, to some extent, the logic of the field with regards to genre and storytelling, they do not need to be able to articulate this logic. A successful series text can therefore be produced via intuitive steps and adapting existing knowledge.

However, just as one may learn the rules and terminology that govern the minutiae of grammar, a writer may choose to assimilate more formal approaches to understanding the mechanics of story, how to navigate the publishing landscape, or which parts of the reading community is most receptive to their genre, style, and narrative voice. The metaphor of grammar also hints at another significant aspect of the logic of the field: just as we can become more conversant with the rules and systems of grammar, said rules and systems are subject to shifts in response to cultural change.

The logic of the field—and an individual agent's understanding of it—has always had poetic implications alongside commercial ones. As Wilkins and Bennett note, the relationship between writer and publisher is often a symbiotic one, as writers need the infrastructure of publishers or their equivalent in emerging distribution formats in order to access their audience (2). A writer has traditionally needed the resources of a publisher to get their work in front of readers, while publishers seek out works by writers to fill their publishing schedule. This symbiosis shapes writers' careers as they come to understand the logic of the field, and shape their work to the market expectations. Certainly, I have felt this in my own practice. As a younger writer—not yet twenty, living on the Gold Coast, with ambitions of writing fantasy—my knowledge of the field suggested my greatest chance of success lay in writing epic fantasy trilogies. They were, after all, the books which appeared on the shelves of my local bookstore and caught the attention of the limited cohort of fantasy writers I knew.

Years later, the advent of electronic submission opened up short fiction markets that had been difficult or impossible to Australian writers to access due to the cost and complexity of international postage. My work adapted to suit the tastes and requirements of the editors of these markets, and in doing so leant into genre elements borrowed from magic realism, post-modern fiction, and hard-boiled crime rather than epic fantasy.

Easy access to overseas submissions proved a pivotal change in the field's logic for me, but fifteen years later, it seems almost inconsequential when weighed against the rapid disruption and evolution of contemporary publishing. Digital books, print on demand, online sales, and social media all represent a new status quo, and the implications of those changes are still being felt. A considerable amount has been written about what has changed, why it has changed, and what it means for the future of writing and publishing. Craig Mod envisions the use of digital tools to create a 'subcompact' magazine market, while Timothy Laquintano has charted the transition from 'vanity' to 'self-publishing', and Mark McGurl charts the changes wrought upon the book by the rise of Amazon. Very little addresses the more interesting question for writers: if the logic of the field can shape the works writers produce, how does this evolving logic of the field impact the way stories are told?

I turn here to the field of television studies, where the interplay between poetics and marketplace has already seen some focus, particularly with regards to disruptive technologies. In *Complex TV*, theorist Jason Mittell explores the growth of complex serial poetics as the dominant narrative form, rejecting the need for plot closure at the end of every episode in favour of the underlying assumption that a television narrative builds up over a seasonal arc (18). Starting in the nineties, these programs have worked against the conventional narrative style of their era, embracing long-term character arcs and the slow build-up of mythology.

Mittell links this poetic evolution to a series of key technological shifts, which changed the constraints normally placed upon television stories (33). This shift began with television series being packaged into DVD boxed sets, allowing the episodes to be consumed in new ways (36). This repackaging also altered the aesthetics of television programs, transforming them from an intangible broadcast to an object to be placed on shelves alongside films and classic novels (36). These transitions allowed viewers more control over how and when they watched —and rewatched—the narrative.

These changed represented a fundamental shift in the logic of the field, and creators saw narrative opportunities in a readership with ready access to repeat viewings of their favourite programs. Complex TV emerges from a shift in how television narratives make meaning, and the guiding question for his poetic analysis lies in understanding "how does this text work?" (Mittell 4-5). In short, Mittell is less concerned with what these changes mean, or how they impact society, and focuses on the creative responses of creators and producers. Or, to borrow Thompson's metaphor, he's seeking to articulate the emerging and evolving rules of television grammar, based upon how the language is being used.

The changes to the logic of the publishing field may be different to those that have brought about Mittell's Complex TV, but I argue they are no less meaningful and have fostered an environment where series fiction gaining popularity as both a publishing strategy and a creative form. As I will argue in coming chapters, seriality is a dominant narrative mode in the self-publishing field, and an increasingly popular one in contemporary fiction publishing. Much has been written about why writers are choosing to write series fiction, and its renewed popularity has seen the emergence of how-to guides and practical discussions about the craft and business of series. Many of these texts focus on how series fiction is different to writing stand-alone fiction, and how their processes have changed or tactical approaches to achieving success with a series. There is an acknowledgement that writing a series is different, but rarely a clear articulation of why it's different or how those differences can be used to productive effect. If the logic of the field can be likened to the rules of grammar, as Thompson suggests (11), there seemed little interest in articulating the rules governing serial fiction in a cohesive way. For many agents within the publishing field—including myself—the logic of series fiction could only be understood in intuitive, rather than formal, ways.

I approached this research as both a small-press publisher, a professional fiction writer, and an academic, engaging in a practice-led approach that seeks to develop a deeper understanding of why series fiction is different to the stand-alone story and how to embrace the series form in pursuit of both creative and professional goals. Although the prospects of laying bare all the aspects of series poetics are intriguing, they remain outside the scope of this book. I do not suggest that my attempts to unearth the logic of the field regarding series fiction is definitive. Instead, it's an attempt to model how the series poetics might be understood and explained. With this in mind, I have approached this research through several methodologies.

First, I produced this research while writing several novellas that used and informed the critical work. Two in particular a mentioned throughout, *White Harbour War* and *Cerberus Station Rumble,* from my Dana Valkyrie Adventure series. Familiarity with thee works is not essential to understanding my argument here, but may provide practical examples of the theory. These works emerged alongside my critical engagement with series poetics, both reflecting and informing my theoretical engagement as I navigated the expectations I brought to the series as well as the expectations of the broader culture. Creative practices are often individual and idiosyncratic, and the aspects of the series under investigation privileged creative issues or instances where I've felt like my understanding of the logic of the field was inadequate.

I also argue these same idiosyncrasies create nuances in the research. As Mittell suggests in his examination of Complex TV, any examination of form acknowledges that it's in dialogue with "cultural contexts, historical formations, and modes of practice" (4), and I come to this research as a practitioner who has been working in digital publishing since 2005. This research weaves insights from my creative work into both relevant scholarship and analysis of other writer's attempts to wrestle with the relevant issue.

Second, I have engaged with academic research on series fiction, using it to develop terminology and processes that allow me to articulate how series fiction operates differently from a stand-alone story and why it matters. Where there is little formal research into the series form, I have supplemented my research by drawing upon nearby fields such as television studies and genre theory where complimentary work and ideas can be found.

Third, I have engaged with resources that articulate how other writers and publishers have been using the series, both inside and outside the speculative fiction genre. These include existing interviews with high-profile authors of series, the emerging body of "how to" guides focused on the series form, reporting, blog posts, and other informal writings laying bare the practical application of series forms with first-hand or second-hand accounts. While not always accurate or broad in scope, these resources represent the practical methods by which many writers develop their awareness of the logic of the field. Engaging with these texts often highlighted gaps in the field's logic, where the assumed knowledge runs counter to my own experiences or understanding.

Each of the chapters that follow interrogates an aspect of series fiction. Chapter one examines some existing perspectives on series fiction and how it functions, interrogating issues of verisimilitude and reader expectations can affect both the creation and consumption of series works. I break down the different approaches to seriality, and draw upon genre theory to suggest series fictions develop into a microcosmic genre within the broader frameworks and reading communities.

Chapter two interrogates issues of temporality within the series, and how technological shifts in the publishing landscape have affected the publication and framing of series works. I look at the emergent language surrounding series works that seek to foreground new approaches to releasing and reading series fiction, and argue that issues of temporality and release schedule influence the experience of reading series fiction.

Chapter three explores the way series works use that temporality to suspend the reader in a state of ellipsis once an individual instalment has ended, and the impact that has on assumed wisdom of character arcs and story progression. Using the work of writer and game designer Robin Laws, I explore an alternate framework for describing characterisation in series fiction, and make the case that the structure of the series itself can be used to poetic effect.

Finally, my conclusion turns towards the emergent interest in series fiction across the publishing field and interrogates what it means to write a successful series. I lay out the shifting landscape against which series works are written and published, how series poetics have adapted to publishing environments, and highlight why the poetic issues described herein are important in both the fields of traditional and self-published fiction. I then conclude with my own critical reflections on my creative response to the issues and queries raised.

STRANGE LIAISONS
UNDERSTANDING SERIES VERISIMILITUDE AND SERIAL CONNECTIONS

I first read Raymond Chandler's novella, "Goldfish", in a now-lost anthology of golden age detective stories. I immediately fell for Chandler's hard-boiled style and his protagonist, Philip Marlowe, and found myself particularly taken by the opening paragraph of the second chapter:

> *The last time I had been in the Gray Lake district I had helped a D.A.'s man named Bernie Ohls shoot a gunman named Poke Andrews. But that was higher up the hill, farther away from the lake. This house was on the second level, in a loop the street made rounding a spur of the hill. It stood on a terrace, with a cracked retaining wall in front and several vacant lots behind.* (Chandler 479)

For years, I assumed it was a throwaway reference—a hint of an in-depth backstory that added a layer of menace to the current investigation but held no overt clues or bearing on the narrative. It became a narrative conceit I used in my own work, evoking a larger world beyond the current story. I longed to capture the same feeling of rich history this throw-away line contained. Years later, after I acquired Everyman's Library collection of Chandler's short fiction, I came to realise the introduction referred to Chandler's short story "Finger Man", first published in a 1934 edition of *Black Mask*.

Chandler's two-line reference to the killing of Poke Andrews offers an interesting lens through which to view series fiction. One doesn't need to understand it refers to a specific story in order to enjoy "Goldfish", and the reference is accompanied by very little contextualising information that might guide a reader towards that earlier story. And yet, discovering the connection created a frisson of pleasure in me as a reader, a confirmation that I'd come to a deeper sense of connection with Chandler's work and the narrative world of Philip Marlowe.

This chapter is concerned with the relationships between series texts, both implied and overt, and how they shape and reshape our readings of series texts. The first part of this chapter explores the ways in which series structures frame the textual connections between individual works, and the different framings imply different relationships and series norms. The second part of this chapter examines how the establishment of norms shapes both the creation and reception of the series itself, building on the work of prominent genre theorists and the productive role reader expectations play in the engagement with the text. I will conclude the chapter by arguing that genre theory, and its associated interest in expectations, makes it possible to treat series fiction as a micro-genre within the broader genre, building its own norms and reading community by making connections between the texts overt.

One of the fundamental pleasures of series fiction lies in the fact the works connect, but how these connections operate and why they're useful are under-explored aspects of writing craft. When reviewing the small selection of literature aimed at writers aspiring to write a series, I found a strong tendency to treat series narratives as prolonged, multi-part stories. Writers are advised to make sure they have a strong meta-plot that will carry over the length of the series, while treating stories themselves as standalones (Daniels ch. 1-ch. 2). Writers are urged construct series bibles that allow for the tracking of arcs and story events

(Wiesnar ch. 4; Palmquist ch. 7), and ensure each series instalment is satisfying as a stand-alone in addition to serving as a waypoint in the series itself (Daniels ch. 2; Wiesnar ch. 2). Much of the field's attention is focused on the fact that the series advances, without considering how and why the narratives may be interconnected. This generates a lack of nuance—to look at a trilogy such as *Lord of the Rings* and conflate the textual relationships between the books with Raymond Chandler's *Philip Marlowe* stories and novels is to overlook the very different expectations of the relationship between the series texts.

The nuances of these relationships are rarely explored, yet its clear readers bring very different expectations to each series regarding how and why events connect. A useful form of framing these expectations can be found in Victor Watson's study of children's and young adult fiction, *Reading Series Fiction: From Arthur Ransome to Gene Kemp*. Here, Watson identifies the two key pleasures that characterises reading a series: first, we get the continuing satisfaction of observing the same characters over a long period, both in the real world and within the ongoing narrative of the series; second, we get the satisfaction of a narrative conclusion in the current text we're reading, even as the series continues (7). For Watson, these acts of resolution are central to the appeal of the serial, distinguishing it from serialised fiction which progresses onwards, each instalment setting up the next. Rather, the series resolves as it proceeds, and this ongoing pattern of completion develops a stability for the reader in the form of breathing space or dramatic closures as the series progresses (7). For the writer, however, this presents a narrative challenge, as the dramatic closure at the conclusion of one story is balanced against the necessity of introducing a dramatic opening in the next.

Watson also introduces an intriguing argument when he explores the implications of these ongoing dramatic closures in children's fiction, suggesting that:

> *A series of novels can express far more subtly than a single novel the ambivalence of age and time which is central to the experience of childhood. The ambivalence arises from a child's*

> *strange and contradictory perception of life as changeless and cyclical, and at the same time as shot through with change; the apparent stability of a predictable sequence of school terms, Christmases and birthdays is forever set against the unstoppable stages of teeth falling out, growing bigger, and experiencing personal and social rites of passage. The characters in a series reflect this: they both do and don't grow older — or they grow older very slowly. (7)*

This positioning of the series is significant because Watson positions the series itself—rather than the individual works—as a poetic device that can achieve a particular effect the stand alone may not. While these effects may be achieved inadvertently, they can also become a tool writers can deploy to further artistic or commercial goals.

While Watson's focus is on the ways existing texts make use of the series format, his work elucidates many of the subtleties that guide the reading of series. In subsequent work, *Series Fiction*, Watson attempts a taxonomy of the series that distinguishes between three dominant approaches—a distinction predicated upon the relationship that's established between component texts. The first of these—the progressive series—foregrounds advancement through texts in a set order as the expected reading experience. In these series, the texts build upon one another and tell an ongoing story in serialised instalments, firmly establishing the chronology and reading as important within the field of significance in each text. To realise that you're reading the first instalment of a progressive series is to shift your expectations as a reader; the story you're reading is going to end, and this end-point should be satisfying, but it is ultimately marked by an ellipsis and the promise that further narrative awaits; the ultimate end-point for the protagonist lies in future volume.

This approach to series and the associated expectations seems to sit at the heart of advice offered by writers such as Penn, Daniels, and Palmquist, and is particularly prevalent in the speculative fiction field where trilogies abound. The progressive relationship between the texts may be made overt through a texts marketing and meta-data, but there are also signifiers within the text itself. George R. R. Martin's *A Song of Fire and Ice*, for example, foregrounds a dominant narrative question the series sets out to answer: who will sit on the Iron Throne of the fictional country of Westeros? Each volume represents a small part of the larger story, frequently tracing characters and events from major disruptions that ask the reader to recontextualise and reorient themselves within the broader story. The first book, *A Game of Thrones*, establishes a disruption to the status quo—the chief advisor of the King, John Arryn, has been killed and northern lord Ned Stark and his extended family are pulled into the political machinations of Westeros politics when Stark is asked to take Arryn's place. This inciting incident triggers a major shift in the political status quo, with Stark discovering evidence that the king's son is a bastard, the king dying on a hunt, while external forces threaten the kingdom in the form of barbarian tribes, the legitimate heir of an overthrown king, and supernatural forces invading from the north. The first book ends with a pivotal event which recontextualises the conflict: Ned Stark is branded a traitor by the bastard heir to thrown, and beheaded, but not before news of his discovery spreads and incites the civil war that will start in the second book.

The second book focuses on the changing lives of viewpoint characters now the war has begun, tracing their path and engagement with various stakeholders in the war for the throne. As with book one, the second book ends with a pivotal event that represents a massive change in context: a pivotal battle fought at the capital of Kings Landing that changes the political landscape as one major contender for the throne is defeated, while Ned Stark's children find themselves on a new circumstances after being scattered by the events at the end of book 1. His eldest son, Rob, is declared King of the North and drawn into a war with the kingdoms to the south who killed his father. Starks bastard son, Jon, is sent north to spy on the Wildling tribes there. His daughter Arya is headed to a foreign land, about to learn the art of assassination from the magical Faceless men, while other Stark children are en route to learn magical in the isolated north, are about to escape capture by the family's enemies, or are in hiding.

In doing this, the series foregrounds for the reader two repeating patterns: individual texts will contain part of the answer to the series central narrative question—who will sit on the throne—and they will chart events between pivotal shifts in the overall narrative. It is reasonable for the reader to expect the central question of who will sit on the Iron Throne to be finalised in the final instalment, foregrounding the progressive continuity of the series as a central pre-occupation. One might read the stories in isolation, but they are designed to flow and build on one-another.

In contrast, Watson also posits the existence of successive series: texts which feature recurring characters, even recurring protagonists, for whom the ongoing development is not the primary concern, and in which the reading order and an individual texts' chronology are not a significant factor. While individual texts may reference events and chronology of other series work, a lack of familiarity will not adversely affect the reading experience. Often tied to this is the assumption that character development is contained within the bounds of the current story, rather than evolving towards a final climactic change. Although these series are often unified by a central character, such as Raymond Chandler's Phillip Marlowe, Lee Child's Jack Reacher, or Agatha Christie's Miss Marple, they can also deploy other unifying elements such as settings, places, or institutions. Such an approach is common in romance series, such as Lauren Dane's contemporary *Brown Family* series or Anne Gracie's *Devil Riders* books, where a different protagonist from the unifying group takes centre stage in each instalment.

While progressive series texts are unified by and work towards the resolution of a communal dramatic question, charting pivotal points in a longer tale, successive books focus on delivering resolution to a dramatic question within each instalment. The central narrative questions of "Goldfish"—where are the stolen Leander pearls and who is killing people to find them?—are introduced in the opening chapters of the story, and resolved in the final chapters. Similarly, Anne Gracie's *Bride by Mistake* introduces the characters of Lieutenant Luke Ripton and the woman who longs for him, Isabella. The question of whether they'll fall in love is introduced and resolved in the space of a single book, even if Ripton appears in earlier *Devil Riders* texts focused on the love lives of other characters.

What unifies these texts is not an ongoing narrative question, or even progressive character development. Lee Child's *Jack Reacher* series is marked by an ongoing reversion to the status quo. Even in books which end with a seeming evolution or change in the character, such as Reacher settling down with love interest Jodie at the end of the third book, *Tripwire*, are undone in the opening chapters of the next volume. In the fourth Reacher novel, *The Visitor*, Jodie dumps him and moves to London to further her career by the end of the first chapter. While the stories of a successive series may be self-contained, this doesn't prevent the series from sharing communal themes, characters, and setting. Further, they often share recurring themes, story beats, and structures: Marlowe, Reacher, and Marple all feature in stories revolving around solving crime, even if their methods are different, while Dane and Gracie explore romantic relationships. In contrast to the progressive series, where each instalment marks a point of recontextualization on the path to resolving an ongoing dramatic question, one might argue the successive series presents thematically similar dramatic questions in a variety of new contexts.

Watson's last category focuses on the format series, "works, often written by a syndicate of authors, bound together by theme, characters or genre, and marketed as a recognisable commodity with its own brand features" (535). A texts status as a format series does not preclude the invocation of other series norms. The series may "aspire to the conditions of either the progressive or the successive series," (535) as seen in the *Nancy Drew* or *Sweet Valley High* novels. Branding may also unify texts that are otherwise unconnected by character or setting, as in the horror-themed *Goosebump* books, Hard Case Crime's hard-boiled pulp crime novels, or Harlequin's *Nocturne* line of paranormal romances. Often, these series rely heavily on generic elements invoked by the trade dress.

Format series which share little more than trade dress and genre raise a complicated question with regards to series poetics:

if all it takes to connect disparate books is a shared approach to design and marketing category, when and how should we consider a book part of a series? The existence of format series such as Orion Publishing's S.F Masterworks, which republishes classic science fiction novels under a shared trade dress and series brand, suggests authorial intentions are not always central to the creation of series works, with series connections forged after publication through the actions of publishers and other agents in publishing who make the connections between the texts implicit. While my interest is primarily focused on texts in which the series aspects of the work are invoked and foregrounded by the author, it is clear series connections are mercurial, with connections beyond narrative that shape their reception.

Although he strives for a taxonomy that can identify disparate approaches to series, Watson isn't blind to the problems of approaching a text with strict taxonomies in mind. He cites the fluidity and volatile nature of series as a complicating element, often making subjects resistant to easy categorisation (535). The apparent predictability of series fiction actually hides a volatility, subject to changes in authorial interest and ongoing feedback (535), and mismatch between the pace in which readers can finish a text and the time needed for writers and publishers to bring the next instalment to market (536). In some cases, an individual text may lie at the intersection of multiple taxonomic categories: R. A. Salvatore's *Streams of Silver* is the second book in his progressive *Icewind Dale* trilogy, later rebranded as the fifth book in *The Legend of Drizzt*. The rebrand established a new, ongoing chronology using prequel books produced after the initial trilogy was a success. All thirty-three novels in the *Legend of Drizzt* are also connected under the format branding of the *Forgotten Realms* setting, originally developed as a role-playing game setting by TSR publishing and still supported by Wizards of the Coast. This branding is shared by over 70 different series works at time of writing, a mix of branded series, progressive, and successive works consisting of over 300 published novels or anthologies in total, plus an additional 16 stand-alone novels ("List of Forgotten"). While Watson's approach cannot claim to classify these works by strict taxonomy, it provides a means for understanding how the authors and publishers deploy the series to achieve specific artistic and commercial effects, and analyse how a particular series interacts with other works that share the branding.

While Watson is one of the first theorists to reconcile the issues of applying a strict taxonomy to volatile texts, broader questions of taxonomy as a tool have been a source of tension within the field of genre fiction and genre theory. Theorists such as Derrida sees genre as patterns of law and transgression, suggesting that genres set limits, and that when a limit is established, norms and interdictions are not far behind (56), but these limitations are only viable when genres are viewed as historic or unchanging categories. Just as Watson's taxonomy fails to neatly categorise Salvatore's *Streams of Silver*, broader genre taxonomies fail to capture the increasingly fluid presentations of genre in the publishing field. They also fail to adequately capture the role genres are by writers and other agents within publishing.

Indeed, for many writers and publishers, genre is not a limitation, but a tool understood as part of the logic of the field. I am very aware of and make use of conventions associated with form and genre in my work as a writer, in both the creation of texts and my attempts to sell them. As the fantasist Neil Gaiman notes, "the advantage of genre is that it gives you something to play to and play against" (Gaiman 405). In his essay "Literary Genres as Norms and Good Habits", literary theorist Thomas Pavel goes so far to suggest that genre is only useful as an interpretive tool because the writer of the text and the culture for whom they were writing used genre as a guideline in the act of creation. Genre norms represent "a successful artistic solution to a representational problem" (209), effectively serving as a guide for writers with similar artistic concerns and desiring similar results. Genres and their conventions become like the conventions of polite behaviour – each rule serves a purpose, and can be ignored, rewritten, or supplanted when that purpose is no longer needed (203). In framing genre in this way, Pavel both emphasises how theories of genre and genre formulation are useful to a writer, and illustrates the drawbacks of taxonomic approach, which can only chart the "polite" works that already exist. The writer's relationship with genre may be polite and unchallenging, but it can also be productive, transgressive, and performative, introducing the same volatility Watson sees in the series by intent. My interest as a writer is not what causes a text to be categorised as science fiction or fantasy, but how and why it is categorised there and what traits I can use to achieve my goals as an artistic and commercial agent within the publishing field. My interest in a series follows a similar progression: I am less interested in what causes a text to be classified as part of a progressive, successive, and format series, and more interested in how those traits are deployed and what those deploying them hope to achieve.

While scholars interested in genre theory may select from a variety of approaches, those which are predicated on providing a strict taxonomy of genre and associated traits are among the least interesting for those of us interested in the craft of writing. In this respect, the branches of genre studies that focus on the how and why texts are positioned—and repositioned—within a particular genre often serve as an unintentional exploration of literary poetics. Theories about the implicit relationship established between texts that fall within a genre such as science fiction, literary fiction, or romance can also model the explicit relationship between series texts. In making these relationships explicit, series texts mimic the effects of genre by establishing expectations and norms which take a productive role in the reader's experience of the text.

The seeds of a reader-centric approach to genre can be found in the work of the Bulgarian structuralist Tzvetan Todorov, whose exploration of genre traits began with the process of decentring the text as the primary source of generic identification, assessed against the list of traits. Instead, Todorov argues that "genres are precisely those relay points by which the work assumes a relationship to the universe of literature" (8), and that genres exist on an abstract level that is separate to the concrete work.

Texts manifest elements of a genre, but do not contain the genre within them. Further, Todorov suggests, "there is no necessity that a work faithfully incarnate it genre, there is only a probability that it will do so" (22). Todorov also expands the classic idea of verisimilitude in relation to genre, moving it beyond the 'naïve' definition that suggests its consistent to reality, and instead exploring 'the relation of the specific text to another, generalised text which is called "common opinion."' (82). This decentring of the text implies genres are unstable and fluid constructs, and invites us, as Kim Wilkins notes in her essay "The Process of Genre", to consider for whom this probability exists. This approach speaks directly to the inherent instability of a series text, which exists as a narrative Schrodinger's cat, both part of a larger narrative and a stand-alone text dependent on expectations brought to bear by the reader. This contradiction informed the hesitation I felt as a writer seeking to produce a sequel—certain creative choices within the text may favour the expectations of a series reader, while others are aimed at a reader who is coming to the series fresh. When those choices suggest contrasting approaches that may alienate the other, I must make decisions about whose expectations hold greater sway.

Further, these decisions must also be negotiated against the potential for future engagement with the series to productively shift the interpretation of a text. In his book, *Towards an Aesthetic of Receptions*, Hans Robert Jauss maintains that critics, writers, and literary historians are "first simply readers before their reflexive relationship to literature can become productive again" (19). Jauss invokes the concept of a 'horizon of expectations' in relation to genre: "The new text evokes for the reader (listener) the horizon of expectations and 'rules of the game' familiar to him from earlier texts, which as such can be varied, extended, corrected, but also transformed, crossed out, or simply reproduced." (88) While Torodorov argues that genres are interactions, Jauss introduces the idea that these interactions take place within a historically specific moment, and that these interactions are subject to shifts over time. This has two important implications for understanding series: the first is the way the horizon of expectations shift once we recognise the series text as a series text, with explicit connection to additional narratives. The connections between each text is a field of significance (Quinn 51) for the reader. The second implication lies in the way this horizon of expectations shapes the way in which textual elements become significant. New texts in a series, much like new texts in a genre, can transform, correct, or extend ideas introduced in prior texts as they re-enter the field of significance, potentially delighting or dismaying readers.

While the notion that the texts is decentred as a means of decentring genre is useful to a writer, alerting us to the ways in which reader expectations shape their reception to a text, it is the theorists who have built upon this foundation that offer the greatest insight into the way they can impact on the creation and reception of series text. I turn here to the works of three theorists in particular: Jonathan Culler's exploration of genre's role in poetics, exploring how genre helps us naturalise the events of a text; Rick Altman's conception of genres as interpretive communities who share a communal approach to arresting the free play of possible signifiers in a particular way; and Kim Wilkins' study of regimes as verisimilitude and their role of positioning a text within a particular genre. All three trace the productive role genre expectations play in the reading and reception of a text, and possess valuable insights into how these same expectations may be manipulated and used in series texts.

Culler explores the role of genre in his book *Structuralist Poetics*, arguing it's the third of five modes of verisimilitude (or vraisemblance) by which a text is naturalised and meaning is assimilated or interpreted by the reader (164) in order to make the text coherent. The layers preceding genre in Culler's model are focused on issues of intelligibility, then cultural influence; a reader may assume a character who begins to laugh will eventually stop, for example, even if the termination of the laughter is not explicitly referenced (165). Similarly, the reader brings culturally coded verisimilitudes and attitudes to the text based upon their experience within, and the assumptions constructed by, the culture they inhabit. These modes of verisimilitude are important, but those of primary interest to us in genre and series poetics lie in the remaining three: generic verisimilitude, the level to which the text obeys generic convention, and finally the level of parody and irony.

For Cuttler, generic verisimilitude occurs as each reader brings a set of literary norms by which a text may be related (169), designating certain kinds of action and assumptions as a shared convention. These conventions can potentially override the reader's expectations drawn from the earlier levels; while it is implausible for a character to laugh forever in the 'real' world, it is not impossible for them to do so in some fantasy settings. More importantly, generic verisimilitude brings with it broader expectations of how the text will behave. Culler identifies hallmarks of the crime genre as "the assumption that all characters are psychologically intelligible, that the crime has a solution that will eventually be revealed, that the relevant evidence will be given but that the solution will be of some complexity." (172). In effect, generic verisimilitude tells us what kinds of problems the genre is likely to present, how they are most likely to be solved, and how they story world is likely to behave. These generic assumptions draw from a broader corpus, building upon the reader's familiarity with other narratives (in general) and other crime narratives (in particular), and bound by the reader's implicit understanding that these texts are unified by conventions of style, theme, and intent. It is on this third level that Watson's attempted taxonomy of the series can be read, with progressive, successive, or format-based approached to unifying a series all suggesting differing models of generic verisimilitude.

Similarly interesting to writers of the series is Culler's fourth level of verisimilitude, the conventionally natural. This level is invoked by texts that use the implicit or explicit identification and avoidance of generic conventions in order to disarm objections against the improbable (173). The text shows an awareness of its own artifice and conventions, "so as to convince the reader that it is aware of other ways of looking at the matter at hand and therefore can be trusted not to distort things while taking its own course" (174). It forces the reader to cast a wider net and include additional genre conventions or texts while interpreting the story (176). For example, an urban fantasy text may invoke the generic conventions of the hard-boiled detective novel in terms of story structure and tone, while alerting the reader to points of divergence through references to fantasy elements in the design, marketing copy, and opening chapters of the text. This invocation of the fantastic alerts readers to the potential for narrative to diverge from the strict psychological intelligibility and realism of the crime genre, signalling the high probability that the fantastic of the uncanny will be involved as the story moves towards its resolution.

This tactic applied to the writing and marketing of my novella, *Horn*, but the level of the conventionally natural also hindered my creation of the sequel. While the implicit connections forged to the fantasy and crime genres set the tone for the reading of the first work, the second would also be read against both the genres and the conventions established within the first text. During the editorial phase of the second book, this resulted in some discussion as how these violations should be handled.

We can see, then, that series texts invoke this level of verisimilitude as soon as the reader knows the text they're reading is part of a series. When reading a series of novels, one is reading both a novel and a series instalment, and we may set aside certain novelistic conventions in service of the series. Series text may also invoke this level, specifically and meaningfully, within the text itself in order to foreground series elements that have little or no bearing on the story being told in the current text.

This intersection can result in some deft handling of series challenges, when deployed by a skilled writer. For example, Charlie Huston's *A Dangerous Man*, the third instalment in his Henry Thompson crime series, foregrounds a two-page recap of the first two novels through a switch from first-person, present-tense narration to a second-person narrative that begins with "This is how you lose your life" (16), treating the recap as its own narrative inside the text. It is one of the most seamless insertions of backstory I've encountered in a series text, evoking the disruption of the novel form. Such recaps may be an expected, established norm within series texts to fill in the gaps for readers encountering the series for the first time, but they are often a disruption to the ongoing flow of the narrative for readers already familiar with the prior texts, revisiting events they already know. Huston is one of the few writers to make the recap itself a meaningful part of the narrative, and he does so by evoking the fifth level of verisimilitude, parody and irony.

For Culler, parody and irony are a highly specialised variant of his fourth level, invoking the conventions of one genre while elevating it to a second level of interpretation, calling attention to the difference and resemblance rather than seeking naturalisation on the new level (178). Huston's recap invites reading as both an artifice of the series, but also as irony. The story elements included are inherently background detail, with little bearing on the story being told in *A Dangerous Man*. Nevertheless, they orientate the text and the reader within the broader continuity of the *Henry Thompson* series. However, Huston positions the opening sequence after the protagonist, Henry Thompson, violently murders a Russian crime boss. He also switches the narration from first person to second person. This both calls attention to the recap's out-of-continuity status with the current story, but also invites us to consider why Henry Thompson has stepped out of his own narration.

Huston uses the second-person mode in order to create distance between the man he is and the man he used to be. Rather than simply orienting the reader within the series, the "you" referred to is identifiably the books narrator, Henry Thompson, using second person narration to create emotional distance between his present and his past. To look back on who he used to be in prior books is painful, and not something he's willing to face head on. In doing so, the recap serves both a narrative purpose beyond merely orienting readers unfamiliar with the prior texts in the series.

While Culler speaks to how genre expectations shape our reception of a text, Rick Altman's study of genre and the American musical invites us to consider how these expectations are formed. In *The American Film Musical*, Rick Altman suggests genres represent interpretive communities, who "arrest the free play of a texts signifiers in a particular way, thus producing a meaning proper to the particular community in question"

(Altman 2). Clarity of meaning in fiction is only possible when author and audience are part of the same interpretive community (2), and genres provide a specific set of intertexts that can serve as a short-hand for that interpretive community (4). As series fiction moves from an implicit relationship between texts to an explicit one, the significance of this genre framework for series writers should be clear. While Culler identifies how genre is used to assimilate the text, Altman's model of interpretive communities—whether formal or informal—represents a means by which an author can predict which textual assumptions will be laid against the text. As writers become part of an interpretive community, such as science fiction, they can learn significant texts and traits which may be played to or against.

The expectations of these interpretive communities shape the "polite" conventions assumed by Pavel's conception of genre, and the rules that Gaiman celebrates working to or against. The explicit relationship between series texts suggests they will build up their own interpretive communities within a broader genre, with readers who are part of the "series" community able to detect shades of meaning that are impossible to a newcomer. For example, the myriad progressive trilogies and successive sub-formats at work under the *Forgotten Realms* branding may seem impenetrable to those outside the interpretive community. Meanwhile, members of the broader Forgotten Realms interpretive community know to bring different series expectations to R.A. Salvatore's *Legend of Drizzt* as a sub-format series, driven by progressive series arcs, and the multi-authored Harpers series which utilises a successive series structure.

The ability to learn and predict genre assumptions within an interpretive community have an obvious benefit to writers seeking commercial or artistic success among the community. It also invites us to consider how these interpretive communities and regimes of verisimilitude build up across series work. Although genres may appear to be neutral constructs, they actually serve an ideological function, serving to "control the audiences action to a specific film by providing the context in which that film must be interpreted" (Altman. 4), and "prejudicing us towards one set of intertexts rather than another…providing and enforcing a pre-reading of the text at hand" (5). In short, they prepare the reader to pull certain elements into the field of significance even before the first page is read. To position a book as romance is to prime our attention for acts of connection of attraction in the opening pages, just as framing a book as fantasy will prime our attention for moments of magic, the uncanny, or wonder in the text. I argue this same process of pre-reading occurs when a reader identifies a work as part of a series, effectively creating a micro-genre which provides a pre-reading of all subsequent texts as series-specific expectations with regards to structure, characterisation, realism, and other narrative traits.

Indeed, this pre-reading is part of the appeal of series texts. We might consider Marie-Laure Ryan's interrogation of storyworlds here, which considers the life of a text after consumption. Ryan argues texts "remain inscribed in our minds long after the signifiers have vanished from memory. This means that story is a cognitive rather than a linguistic construct." These storyworlds exist beyond the text, as evidenced by the tendency for a story to proliferate across multiple formats and adaptations. When noting the proliferation of transmedia franchises, including series texts such as *Lord of the Rings* and *A Game OF Thrones* making their move from fiction to film and other mediums, Ryan and Thon note part of the appeal of the franchise lies in the instant immersion it provides, "because the recipient is spared the cognitive effort of building a world and its inhabitants from a largely blank state" (1). The promise of a series is that the storyworld not only lives as a cognitive construct, but expands with subsequent releases. The same storyworld construct which make series texts an appealing option for proliferation for other media also offers also presents intriguing possibilities for authors of series texts.

The notion of series fans forming a subculture within broader genre categories is one that has been explored within studies of fan culture. Indeed, series fictions have a long history of growing micro-communities within a broader genre—a phenomenon I will explore further in Chapter 2, tracing the possibility that the series actually encourages the formation of these communities, because readers treat every narrative endpoint as an ellipsis rather than a full-stop. What's often neglected is the effect that these micro-genre expectations can have on the act of writing, whether conscious or subconscious. Just as Gaiman sees genre expectations as a playground, an astute writer can play to the expectations set by earlier works in their series. So long as we understand those expectations, they can be fulfilled or subverted with specific intent. This is particularly true as a series grows, creating additional explicit connections that reinforce those expectations and establish the regime of verisimilitude at work in the series texts.

This does not imply that verisimilitude is necessarily easy to predict, however. While Culler uses verisimilitude to explore how a text is naturalised and understood, and Altman provides a framework for understanding how those expectations can be learned and understood by a writer working in genre spaces, it is Kim Wilkins work on the role genre plays in the positioning and valuing of a text that holds powerful implications for a series writer.

Wilkins explores how stakeholders involved in the creation, publication, and promotion of her novel *Giants of the Frost* positioned and re-positioned the genre of her work, sometimes working against authorial intentions. Building on the works Jauss and Culler, Wilkins argues for the existence of "regimes of verisimilitude" at work in every genre, establishing levels of possibility and plausibility based upon "what is commonly held to be true for that genre at that time." (Wilkins). These regimes of verisimilitude are "formed, negotiated, and reformed, both tacitly and explicitly, by the interactions of authors, readers, and (importantly) institutions." The repositioning of Wilkins' work from the genre of fantasy to romance by some publishers and readers impacted both the reception and value of the work within those interpretive communities. These shifts are significant, particularly for writers of a series, as it implies that the regimes of verisimilitude are not entirely within the writer's control.

Written as a commercial fantasy novel and the creative component of her PhD, *Giants of the Frost* intentionally catered to two different interpretive communities. As such, Wilkin's account shows, "that there were negations and renegotiations over what genre Giants is, but also that there are continual negotiations and renegotiations over which elements (in specific moments) constitute which genre" (Wilkins). This is especially true once the novel was classified as romance in some markets against authorial intent. In circumstances where the text ran counter to the regime of verisimilitude associated with a genre—notably, the lack of romance's happily ever after—the failure to meet these expectations resulted in negative reader responses with subsequent commercial implications.

Wilkins' experiences are a potential warning to series authors. The regimes of verisimilitude established by the explicit connections between series texts are both a powerful tool for writers, but also a potential danger. As Wilkins has shown, a failure to meet these expectations are component of both reader satisfaction and narrative success, but they aren't always within the author's control. It behoves series authors to not only be conscious of the horizon of expectations they establish with their series works, and how those expectations play to or against their broader genre, but also those brought to the series by the series readership. Series authors should, I argue, be very conscious of the series potential to form a very specific micro-genre and the associated expectations brought to the work by readers, which both shape the reception of the text and offer writers a useful tool.

Authors are not bound by genre, but the logic of the field suggests they are mindful of genre concerns when they write. As Gaiman suggests, the norms of these genres are something to work to and against, while Pavel's foregrounds the productive role genre plays in the creation of text. However, they are not the final arbiter of how and where their texts may be positioned. Wilkins experiences showcase the ways in which genres are procedural rather than taxonomic, reliant on the positioning of stakeholders beyond the author, including the broader readership, publishers, and other institutions that interact with the text. These textual associations matter, and shape the writers craft, and they are mirrored in the shared connection between series stories. While I do not wish to suggest that series texts make up a genre unto themselves, it's my contention the series creates its own micro-regime of verisimilitude within the broader genres in which it's positioned, a micro-regime formed upon reading a first text in the series and then extrapolating outwards when the reader learns additional texts may exist under the series banner. These expectations draw series elements into the field of significance for the reader, just as recognised genre traits do. To borrow the phrasing of Pavel, there becomes a polite way of continuing a series, and an impolite method of doing so, based on the interpretive community and the association the reader brings to the text.

In the introductory chapter, I referenced Thompson's concept of the logic of the field, which describes the procedures agents use to generate effects within publishing. Such knowledge may be intuitive, but it does not prevent a writer from recognising their understanding of the field is flawed. I felt this acutely in my early series works, and in Watson's taxonomy of series types and Wilkin's procedural approach to genre, I found a frame that allowed me to understand my own intuitive discomfort.

Wilkins' experiences with *Giants of the Frost* and its movement between interpretive communities suggests both genre and the communities that surround them are part of the logic of the field that writers, publishers, and other agents utilise when positioning a creative work for success. The regimes of verisimilitude these connections bring to bear on a text can provoke both positive and negative reactions from readers, especially when expectations are thwarted.

Altman's model of interpretive communities is interesting to consider here: with each additional work in a series, the writer is no longer catering to an interpretive community guided by genre, but a second interpretive community guided by their familiarity with prior works in the series. It's here that my intuitive discomfort with writing series fiction prior to undertaking this research finds a logic I can articulate. The experienced series reader and those coming to the text for the first time represent two different interpretive communities, each working with a different array of texts brought within the field of significance. Catering to one means acting in ways that can be considered "impolite" to the other.

Although series texts are not genres, as many theorists think of them, the explicit connections made when works are grouped together under an overarching series brand can suggest connections in the eyes of writers and readers. These connections establish series expectations that mimic the processes of genre, and open up the same possibilities for subverting, fulfilling, or repositioning as a broader genre expectation. In deploying Watsons analysis of series structure, I wish to sidestep the issues inherent in strict taxonomy. Rather, his analysis identifies a trio of procedural prototypes that govern the way series works connect to one another—established precedents readers can understand on an intuitive level, which a writer may then cleave to in the name of simplicity or intermingle to create complexity. There is little to prevent an episodic series from establishing a short, progressive arc, nor a progressive series from setting aside its ongoing story to engage in a short side-story of interest to readers.

Watson's taxonomy also suggests how series connections themselves are part of the horizon of expectations. They strongly suggest what the serial connections in a series mean regarding the horizon of expectations, and how significant those connections may be. Chandler's reference to Poke Andrews in "Goldfish" is a momentary connection in otherwise stand-alone, successive narratives, only likely to be caught by an interpretive community familiar with the "Finger Man" text. In a progressive series narrative, where Marlowe would push towards a particular endpoint in later books that mark the "end" of the series, the reference would read differently and might well send the reader in search of prior texts.

When I began work on the Dana Valkyrie stories, my first port of call was examining my prior experiences with series fiction through the lens of my research. While I knew on an intuitive level that I found writing series fiction uncomfortable, Watson's taxonomies and productive approaches to genre theory provide a framework for understanding why. Often, issues of verisimilitude and expectations have always come to the fore—to echo Salesses, issues of craft and expectations are intertwined, and Watson's framework for series forms suggested both a means of understanding the expectations of series of fiction in play.

When I submitted the sequel to *Horn* to my publisher at Twelfth Planet Press, one of the first editorial reactions revolved around my own inability to understand which model of seriality to employ. I'd drafted *Horn* as a stand-alone work, the character's backstory and narrative rhythms designed to reach a point of emotional catharsis and character evolution. In propelling the character into a new story—in effect, triggering a new narrative arc—there was considerable negotiation with my editor about what needed to be replicated, what could fall by the wayside, and what felt like it was missing from the second text. While we were conscious of this break for some readers, others slipped under our radar.

Intuitively, both my editor and I understand the complications of series work, but this didn't help us resolve them. It's only looking back through the filter of Watson's series taxonomy that I can see our challenges: *Horn* had reached a narrative end-point, yet that end-point suggested a dramatic recontextualization of the protagonists status quo, which often signalled a progressive arc. Accounting for this in the second book, which focused on a self-contained case, struck me as clumsy, yet ignoring it felt like a betrayal of the readers who'd followed the series from book 1.

At the same time, both *Horn* and *Bleed* evoked overt genre connections in both style and the framing of the text, using Raymond Chandler's *Philip Marlowe* stories as a touchpoint. Evoking these connections, both overtly and subtly, served as a reference point for reader expectations with regard to genre, but also the successive approach to series Chandler used in Marlowe's narratives. While approaching the story and packaging the book as urban fantasy foregrounded the violation of the generic conventions of the hard-boiled detective novel, but there was no overt signal to readers that the series had embraced a more dramatic, progressive approach.

Bleed is a far stronger book than its predecessor in terms of characterisation and story arc, but a weaker series instalment. Without a clear understanding of the expectations laid against progressive and series works, I tried to write a text which satisfied the norms of both, and ultimately failed. To paraphrase Altman, I failed to arrest the free play of the textual signifiers around the work in a way that allowed me to predict reader expectations and tell a "polite" version of the story, and my ability to tell a meaningful story was compromised.

In contrast, the Dana Valkyrie series began with a clear vision of the recurring structures, tropes, and intertextual allusions I wanted to draw into the field of significance. Each novella would build towards an MMA fight in a different science fiction setting, with story complications providing a shifting context and framework for interrogating the character and conceit. Book one presented Dana being drawn into a fight against her will on a planet that frowns on MMA and brawling, while subsequent books featured Dana fighting to save an old friend of the Captains from a gang (book 2), as a proxy guiding the movements of a giant robot (Book 3), against a woman who hold a grudge against the captain on a water planet (book 4), and against the one woman to hold a victory over Dana who wishes a rematch (book 5). Further iterations are drawn from a list of new contexts that were prepared as the series developed, featuring locations (prison planet, over the rings of Saturn), situations (during a pirate raid, legitimate fight for a title), and character hooks (Dana's mother shows up). A mild continuity is established, but not central to the resolution of each text.

Similarly, the series plan features a list of key character relationship with the supporting cast of Big Wade, Zadie Jayne, and Captain Rackham to be expanded upon in every novella, plus semi-regular characters such as the doctor who joins the crew in book 2, and recurring plot elements such as trouble with the Security Division, Captain Rackham's mysterious past, the galactic diaspora taking place in the books setting, and trouble with local underworld figures.

The repeated patterns of the first five books also suggest a "polite" pattern for a Dana Valkyrie book: Dana arrives on a planet or space station and becomes embroiled in local trouble that can only be resolved by engaging in a legal or illegal fight. The intentional repetition of this structure is designed to set the series norms, which open up possible variations in future texts, such as setting an entire novella on the Viking Maiden or in the slip-space. These variations of the norm represent an intriguing departure from series norms for ongoing readers, while also providing a detailed engagement with two settings which allow the reader to see those locations in a new light.

Further, I began the Dana Valkyrie series with a firm decision about the series archetype I wished to invoke. Like *Horn* and *Bleed*, the Dana Valkyrie stories owe a creative debt to a series of short stories produced in the pulp era: Robert E. Howard's Sailor Steve Costigan stories about a boxing merchant sailor which appeared in magazines in the early 1930s. Like Chandler's *Marlowe* stories, Howard's tales are a successive series, each designed to stand alone but gradually building a shared cast and setting with each instalment. The Dana Valkyrie stories transplants the basic conceit of Howard's character into a new genre—science fiction—and approach each instalment as a novella rather than a short story, but owe a debt to Howard's narrative voice.

In doing so, I'm overtly flying in the face of much advice aimed at series authors. The Dana Valkyrie stories do not progress to an end-point, nor is there a meta-plot connecting each instalment. Those connections which do exist are tangential to the story, much like Chandler's reference to Poke Andrews' death in "Goldfish" serves to connect the story to "Finger Man" without making the works dependent on one-another. While a series continuity exists—astute readers may identify progression through details such as Valkyrie's win-loss record, or Doc Lightner joining the crew at the end of book 2—there's no central narrative question driving the story forward. Similarly, some elements—such as the Dana's family history or Captain

Rackham's past—are focal points of some narratives, while merely informing others without being a focal point or even a passing reference.

While this clarity made drafting easier—I know which audience's concerns and horizon of expectations hold sway when making narrative decisions—it also raised intriguing questions regarding the craft and structure of each story. As both a writer and a writing educator, I'd long worked under the assumption that stories are about characters who change and evolve over the course of the narrative, building towards a moment of moral choice at the climax of their story. Stories are, in effect, transformative for the protagonist, even if they're tragedies where the protagonist refuses to transform.

This approach—often framed as the story's character arc—is satisfying in a stand-alone tale, but creates an intriguing proposition for serial characters who must sustain multiple books or stories. This is especially true for successive series built around a single hero, whose series can extend well beyond the familiar three or seven book arcs we've come to expect from progressive narratives in science fiction or fantasy. Howard wrote 20 *Sailor Steve Costigan* stories, and popular modern examples of successive seriality such as Lee Child's *Jack Reacher* series include over 29 books at a time of writing, although Child handed over the rights and authorship of his character to his younger brother Andrew after the 24th novel (Rawlinson). For these characters to engage in a process of growth and change seems implausible, but also increases the odds that prior works become drawn into the field of significance associated with the series.

To learn to write series, then, does not merely require an understanding of series processes, but how those processes challenge fundamental assumptions about the way stories are told. In the coming chapters, I will explore two issues which are central to understanding this assumptions, starting with the temporal issues that govern the series reading experience in chapter two. This is followed by an interrogation of characterisation in chapter three, seeking a deeper understanding of how characters may be rendered complex and engaging without transformative character arcs.

THIS IS NOT AN ENDING
SERIES TEMPORALITY AND PUBLISHING CONTEXTS

In their 2013 guide to independent publishing, *Write, Publish, Repeat*, authors Sean Platt and Johnny B. Truant advocated for the use of phrases like "Season" and "Episodes" to discuss their series works to give readers an "immediate shorthand, telling them exactly what to expect" (17) regarding series continuity and progression. At the time this terminology was used to describe their weekly publishing schedule, attempting to establish a reading habit among their readers (72), but as described in their follow-up publishing guide, *Iterate and Optimize*, the terminology stuck even when they moved to releasing the whole season in a single release (ch. 9). Even when released as a single narrative document, the components parts were still framed as individual episodes brought together into a curated, season-long whole.

While it can be tempting to dismiss this phrasing as a marketing decision by a pair of canny self-published authors, I argue Platt and Truant are part of a wider trend of rethinking the poetics of the fiction series to incorporate the strengths of a digital publishing environment. In doing so, the interplay between market conditions and the craft of the series take on a productive role, as the ability to access the entirety of a series is often governed by issues of access and temporality. In using television terminology, Platt and Truant invite their readers to rethink their assumptions around both the pace of releases and the relationship between the component texts in their series, resetting expectations among the reading community. In this chapter, I will lay out the nuanced relationship between time and the consumption of series fiction, and how the emergence of digital publishing has changed both the marketing and craft of series fiction. Further, I will argue this changing landscape creates new opportunities to understand and evolve the poetic approaches that underpin series fiction.

While Platt and Truant claim to the forerunners of using the terminology of broadcast television to describe their approach to publishing (17), they are hardly alone in co-opting television terminology to describe publishing projects. These days, independent publishers frequently describe their collected series as boxed sets rather than omnibus editions, and series narratives are discussed in terms of seasonal arcs. However, this is not merely an independent publishing phenomenon. In 2014, the traditional publishing house Farrar, Straus, & Giroux experimented with their own version of this rapid release, upending their traditional publishing cycle in order to release all three volumes in Jeff VanderMeer's Area X trilogy in the space of 8 months (Bosman). Meanwhile, in 2015, the emerging Serial Box publishing house positioned themselves as "HBO for readers" (Reid). Not content to merely co-opt the language of television serials, Serial Box have also taken the production model: each serial is produced by a collaborative writer's room who build the season-long arc under the guidance of a dedicated showrunner, then break up to produce individual novellas that are released weekly in eBook and audio book via a dedicated app alongside eBook "episodes" distributed via distribution channels such as Amazon and Kobo. In all these cases, the use of television technology is an overt signal that the traditional cycles of publishing—typically focused on one or two releases over the course of a twelve-month period—will be disrupted, and the ongoing seriality of the projects are put into focus.

Perhaps the projects are doing nothing new. Serial publications in periodicals have been around since the seventeenth century, rising in popularity throughout the Victorian era (Law). In his autobiography of his experiences as a pulp author, Frank Gruber charts the enormous appetite for work required to keep the pulp magazines alive:

> The average pulp magazine of one hundred twenty-eight pages contained sixty-five thousand words. Since many of the magazines, such as Argosy, Detective Fiction Weekly, Love Story, Western Story, Wild West Weekly, were weeklies, the total market for stories was considerably greater than one hundred fifty times sixty-five thousand words (24-24).

Not all these stories were serials, or even series characters, but potential seriality was a goal of many writer. In their study of Erle Stanley Gardner, Roberta and Francis Fugate note "the lifeblood of the pulps and slicks of the 1920s, '30s, and '40s was continuing characters and serials which accumulated a reader following to bring an increasing number of readers back from one issue to the next," making note that many writers—including the highly prolific Gardner—sought to create recurring characters so popular they became indispensable to the magazine (Chapter 10). In an era where the magazine's success relied on its ability to draw readers eyeballs towards the advertising which ran alongside the stories, the promise of recurring characters and continuing stories were popular marketing tactics.

This is not true of every era. Prose serials became antiquated in the publishing environment of the late twentieth century, aside from a few high-profile projects like Stephen King's 1996 serial *The Green Mile*, which sparked a succession of similar projects from VC Andrews and John Saul (Hendrix). These projects were notable for being exceptions to prevailing publishing norms, and unlike the regular releases of Platt and Truant, the approach was not widely adopted and replicated outside of small experiments. Also noticeable is the pace of publication: King released his serial in monthly print instalments, while author such as Platt and Truant worked off an accelerated weekly release schedule that owed more to the current home of serialised narrative in the twenty-first century, the television series.

While the pace of these releases is significant, the longevity of the series they produce is also worthy of consideration. The popularity of series fiction and characters has often waxed and waned with publishing conditions, and while it's never disappeared from the publishing sphere, the longevity of the series is often governed by market forces. I turn here, briefly, to the field of film and television studies where the productive role the market plays on creative poetics has been done. The film theorist David Bordwell suggests that any study of film poetics must be read against two principal areas of inquiry. The first of these, analytical poetics, deals with matters of construction and achieving particular effects within the work. The second, historical poetics, which asks "How and why have these principles arisen and changed in particular empirical circumstances" (23). Bordwell uses this to frame the interplay between industry and technological norms and the creative practice of filmmakers. The creative choices of the artist are influenced by the prevailing wisdom of their culture and era.

To look at the poetics of the series in 2023 is to examine a resurgent form of fiction. To maintain a long-running series requires ongoing interest from the author, a readership willing to purchase new works, and a publisher willing to make those works accessible. While seriality has always been possible within the publishing field, it has not always been a viable strategy for authors or publisher outside of a handful of best-sellers capable of sustaining sales over a long series. Although much is made of the commercial disruption to the marketplace caused by Amazon, internet technologies, and the rise of the eBook, these discussions rarely embrace the poetic impacts of these shifts. I would suggest that this type of accelerated release schedule independent authors is not just a commercial shift, but an opportunity to utilise the strengths of the series in ways that have not been viable for several decades.

Writers frequently make strategic decisions within the publishing field, although they may not be made consciously. While Roland Barthes may argue for the removal of the author as the dominant arbiter of meaning in a text, an experienced writer is unlikely to be approaching the creation of the text blind to the way their work is likely to be interpreted and released, and choose to preference particular modes of interpretation within particular reading communities. In his 1982 book, *How Literature Works: The Nature of the Literary Experience*, literary theorist Kenneth Quinn posits the existence of a field of significance negotiated between reader and text, an interchange in which a responsive object (the reader's mind and attention) responds to the changing cues and signposts within the text. In particular, Quinn draws attention to the role the text plays in this formulation:

> *The field of significance is something that exists only in the reader's mind. And yet, the starting point, the stimulus to react, is built into the words themselves. As we move along the lines of narrative, the text reaches out to particular areas of our minds, draws ideas to the surface of consciousness as we read.* (52)

This field of significance adapts and adjusts as the reader advances through the text, based upon the connections made and the associations deemed to be meaningful by the reader's experience. Quinn likens the text to a tour guide through a palace, proscribing a path through the terrain with no control over what is observed, which corridors are glanced down or doors opened. Although a reader may linger or study at will, they must also "submit to the forward momentum of the text," or "risk losing the thread" (52). In doing so, Quinn opens the possibility of both good faith and bad faith readings of the text, predicated upon aspects drawn into the field of significance by the writer, publisher, and other agents within the publishing field. Once genre or seriality is invoked within the field of significance, they will play a productive role in the interpretation of the text. Indeed, even if the reader isn't entirely aware that said norms exist, the suggestion they might be plays a productive role in the reading experience.

With this in mind, it's intriguing to consider Quinn's framing in light of the fluid nature of genre and its interpretive communities advocated for by many theorists. While Pavel frames genre as a series of norms and Altman examines genre through the interpretive communalities which build up around them, Quinn's framing invokes a methodology for understanding how these norms and communities come into existence. Agents active in the field – whether writer, publisher, or reader – have a myriad of tools for drawing genre and series elements into the field of significance. These include, but are not limited to, the style and narrative voice used, the opening framing of the story, and genre tropes employed, through to the title development, design, and marketing of the text.

While genre is often brought into the field of significance through informal connection, invoking the overt connection between series texts allows them to establish their own microcosm of norms within their reading community. However, the issue of temporality also plays a role within this microcosm of genre forming around the works. The temporal gap between each instalment in series work represents a potential disruption to the forward momentum and thread of the series—a chance to forget significant elements—while series released quickly or with a long list of instalments offer a greater chance of recognising and normalising series elements drawn into the zone of significance.

These gaps are meaningful because the pleasure of the fiction series is, at heart, a temporal one. As a reader, we know that the final line of a series work is not a full stop, but an ellipsis. This story may stop, as all stories do, but the characters continue on and we will resume their narrative in future volumes as they reach a new series of narratively meaningful events. As Victor Watson frames it, we get "the continued satisfaction of observing the same characters over a long period of fictional and real time" (7). Capitalising on this satisfaction often means pulling the continuing nature of the series into the field of significance, but the commercial realities of the publishing marketplace have often made such decisions risky. The production cycles of traditional publishing and brick-and-mortar stores, which frequently meant a year or more of "real time" between series instalments, made fully capitalising on the seriality of series works a tricky perspective. Worse, access to prior works in a series was often limited by industry realities, including limited bookshelf space at vendors and warehouse storage. This often presented itself in a lack of overt series branding on the publisher's side, with series texts presenting a cataloguing problem for libraries, as "there may be nothing on the cover or title page of the book to alert readers that the book is part of a series" (Nimmo 4). The serial nature of the work may be framed by unifying trade dress and industry norms, but rarely in the official meta-data, and individual releases must also standalone as creative works if read separately from the ongoing series.

Similarly, the serial elements of periodical stories were often limited by the commercial realities of the era. As editor Nick Mamatas (2011) notes, magazine content was paid for by advertising, which meant "magazine content is designed to be disposable, so that the artifact can be freed up to be examined by more people, thus exposing the ads—and the magazine itself—to a wider audience" (61). Thus, the fiction content had to resist rereading, making the "well tied bow" ending a feature of published works (61). As fiction magazines moved online, and thus readers needed to be pulled to the content via shared links, endings with a ragged edge that inspired shares and discussion became a powerful feature.

To develop experience within the field of publishing is to become adept at identifying para-textual and meta-textual queues that can guide reader expectations when picking up a book and editorial tastes when selecting works to publish, in addition to deploying allusions and stylistic queues within the text itself. To write successfully is often an exercise is adapting and deploying traits regarded as significant or valuable by other agents within the field and deploying them in your own work. In short, writers come to understand the norms of their genre, and deploy them towards strategic goals.

With this in mind, the adoption of terms more closely associated with television series to describe prose works is indicative of a shift in the norms of the series in the contemporary publishing landscape. The agents using these terms are drawing the seriality of the work into the field of significance, but they also foreground the idea that these texts will not play to publishing industry norms. Rather than the seriality of the text being hinted at in design choices, the interconnected nature is pulled into the field of signific, and the reader is invited to assume a significantly faster rate of publication of new texts.

The use of television terminology around prose fiction is also intriguing because television poetics themselves have recently undergone a profound shift as a result of changes within the marketplace. In *Complex TV* (2015), Jason Mittell expands on Bordwell's concept of historical poetics and advocates for an approach to poetics that incorporates the way the norms and practices of the television industry, audience, critics, and creators shape the storytelling practices of the medium (5). Significantly, he posits the emergence of a new television poetics because of the impact that technological shifts have made in the way television stories are told, in which "the serial text itself is less of a linear storytelling object than a sprawling library of narrative content that might be consumed via a wide range of practices, sequences, fragments, moments, choices, and repetitions" (7). Central to his argument is the idea that shifts in how television is distributed and consumed, over the last two decades, via the adoption of DVD boxed sets and streaming technology, has resulted in an increased complexity in the poetics of television narrative. I contend that a similar change is occurring in the broader fiction market, albeit driven by very different technological shifts, and the co-option of television terms to describe the norms of a fiction series comes as fiction writers are given the opportunity to control and manipulate the temporal streams that surround fiction works.

Issues of temporality tend to be central to television and film narrative, as their running time is codified and repeatable, especially compared with reading fiction. While Victor Watson identifies fictional and the passage of real-world time at work in the reception of a series, Mittell argues that "seriality itself is defined by time," with the essential form of the series reliant on the parcelling out of story instalments with gaps between the entries (p 27). He goes on to posit three separate temporal streams at work in every story, which provide an intriguing frame for considering both television and prose fiction narratives.

The first temporal stream, Story Time, is used to connote the passage of time within the diegesis of the story world (p 26). Typically, this will be the most straight-forward chronology at work within the story, as characters experience time in their story world via a familiar linear progression, unless there are speculative tropes such as time travel in play.

The second temporal structure in play is the series Discourse Time, which represents "the temporal structure and duration of the story as told within a given narrative, which almost always differs from story time via ellipses skipping over uneventful moments" (p 26). This temporal stream is often at the behest of poetic decisions: events may be reordered via flashback or repeated from multiple perspectives, and the temporal stream of the story-world is manipulated in order to create tension and narrative momentum. In short, discourse time represents the authorial imposition of plot and structure upon the temporal stream of the story time, cherry picking the moments that can be shaped and manipulated in order to generate literary effect.

The power of these manipulations is readily familiar to established writers, whether it is from structural guides to story or EM Forster's oft-quoted distinction between story and plot, which places the emphasis on causality (82). For Forster, the distinction lies in the requests made to the reader: story make invoke curiosity, but plot invokes the reader's intelligence and memory. Plot is an invitation to pick up details and relate it to other facts read in the text (83). This places demands on the writer: "The plot-maker expects us to remember, we expect him to leave no loose ends" (84). It is the decisions the author makes around discourse time that draw narrative events into the field of significance for the reader and make their association meaningful.

The prevalence of countless writers' guides focused on plotting and story structure suggests this aspect of the writer's craft is a challenge in stand-alone novels or stories. However, this challenge is exacerbated when the author commits to a series. The discourse time is not limited to a single narrative, but multiple interconnected narratives that exist within the diegesis of the story world. The unease I felt writing series texts frequently stemmed from this notion of significance within discourse time, and in particular, the line at which familiarity with other series texts was required to submit to the forward momentum of a story and follow its threads to the conclusion. Although a stand-alone text may establish implicit relationships with other texts through allusions, mimicry of narrative styles, or positioning within a genre, labelling a story or novel as part of a series constructs an explicit relationship between them. Even in instances where the reader is unfamiliar with other works, the existence of other series texts shapes the reading experience.

The series writer negotiates two distinctly different fields on behalf of the reader while constructing the text: one in which familiarity with prior texts can lend more significance to minor narrative elements, and a field in which the reader is coming to the series fresh and unaware of significance of those same elements. A single story is a self-contained unit. When it calls back on prior events, the readers interest and memory need only extend to events within the same text. In contrast, series works may call back to events in other series texts, and there is no guarantee a reader of the current text has read, or remembered, the events of prior stories. To write series is to seek a balance between both potential readerships: providing enough information to the new reader to bring series characters and structures into the field of significance, without alienating those readers with the repetition of elements they are already aware of.

This challenge is further exacerbated by the third temporal stream at work in Jason Mittell's model of series, narration time. For Mittell, narration time provides the most enduring method of recognising a series narrative, based upon the alternation between episodic instalments and the temporal gaps between them. He believes that "it's the gaps that define the serial experience," marking the points between discrete narratives and inviting the reader to continue their engagement (27). It would be disingenuous to suggest that the narration time of fiction and television function in the same way. Television has a history of highly codified structures that govern narration time—frequently governed by timeslot and expected episode lengths. (25). In contrast, two different readers may progress through the same fiction narrative at very different paces, pause at very different points, and have traditionally had more opportunities to re-read and re-engage with a narrative.

However, to disregard the effects of narration time on the fiction series because of these differences overlooks factors that affect how fiction is read: while readers have considerably more freedom in how and when the access—or re-access—a fiction text, their engagement is still mediated by the narrative form and external market forces. For example, I first encountered one of J. Gregory Keyes *Fool Wolf* short stories in the pages of *Dragon Magazine 249* in 1998, and realised the story was part of a series upon finding subsequent stories in later issues. It would be another ten years before a collected volume, *The Hounds of Ash and Other Tales of Fool Wolf*, released under the name Greg Keyes, which gave me access to the character's full saga. The collection afforded me the opportunity to see connection between stories I hadn't made when reading in individual issues, but also included additional stories initially released in magazine's I hadn't read. Similarly, after picking the first novel in C.S Friedman's *Coldfire Trilogy* as a young reader, it would take several years of searching second-hand bookstores to find the second volume, and only the emergence of Amazon made it possible to find the third.

While the discourse time involved in reading a story or novel remains variable, the profound shift in the publishing landscape towards ready access to backlist titles is a pivotal change for series poetics. While writing a series once involved managing the risk that some instalments would be inaccessible due to market factors, the rise of eBooks, digital bookstores, and print-on-demand technology have made access to all texts increasingly possible and probable. This shift represents a profound opportunity, both creatively and commercially, and the changing norms of series poetics are responding in kind.

When contemplating the scope of the creative work accompanying this thesis, I found it was also important to consider the role narration time plays around shorter fiction works. A key decision when contemplating creative approaches that would fit within the expected wordcount of a creative thesis was whether to craft a full series of short fiction stories, or an incomplete series of novellas. When weighing up the potential options, a second important aspect of fiction's narration time soon became clear: fiction works, especially short fiction, are often repackaged and re-presented to their audiences, potentially drawing different genres and forms into the field of significance. For example, I first encountered Kim Newman's Diogenes Club stories when 'Egyptian Avenue' was reprinted in *The Mammoth Book of Best New Horror 14*, where Newman characterises the story as "an entry in a series of 1970s-set occult/SF/mystery stories I've been working on" (330) in his preface. As a reader, my experience with the story was heightened by the knowledge future instalments may yet occur, and I began to seek out additional entries. This search drew additional genres into the series Field of Significance. I found a story collected again in *The Years Best Fantasy & Horror: Sixteenth Annual Collection* (2003). Another instalment in the series, 'Soho Golem', was originally published in *Sci Fiction*, reprinted in *The Mammoth Book of Best New Horror 16*, and nominated in the best new novella category of the World Fantasy Awards in 2005 (Title: Soho Golem) before finding its way into the same collection. When the individual stories were later published as a collection in 2006, they were repositioned again, with trade dress positioning the book alongside psychedelic 70s occult mystery television shows which inspired Newman to write the stories. As a reader, the collection itself became significant to my reading experience, as I'd been anticipating a collection and access to stories I'd not yet encountered. This aspect of seriality is difficult to replicate when the texts are presented as a single collection first, while presenting works as a collected text can imply finality and closure to a series, given that preponderance of stand-alone texts whose narratives end at the close of a book. While my experience with short fiction series such as Newman's piqued my interest in this program, I suspected the collection make take a stronger position in the field of significance than the seriality of the stories.

More significantly, the reposition of Newman's work brings a focus on the way fiction series once relied heavily on favourable market and production forces. I first encountered Newman's work in reprint anthologies, and while the speed of his production was prodigious for the era, my engagement relied upon editions within the field championing the series and bringing it to the forefront. One considerable challenge of producing series fiction has been the inherent volatility of the format. As Victor Watson notes:

A series may be written over a period of many years, perhaps covering most of a writer's professional life. In that time the authorial interest is likely to change direction and the later writing will be done with a consciousness of public feedback. (525)

Further, the market itself often precluded series fiction from reaching a firm conclusion. A quick perusal of my own shelves reveals multiple discontinued series that were victim of poor early sales: Cherie Priest's *Cheshire Red* series (Priest) and Melanie Rawn's *Spellbinder* were dropped (Whitehead) and left unfinished because of poor sales of the first two volumes. Intriguingly, the contemporary publishing environment has allowed some series to re-emerge after meeting this fate: the third volume of Joanne Anderton's Veiled Words series, *Guardian*, was dropped by British publisher Angry Robot, only to be "rescued by Tehani and Fablecroft publishing so that Guardian could see the light of day" (Anderton). Similarly, American author Tobias Buckell used a Kickstarter to fund the final volume of his Xenowealth saga (Buckell), albeit after a long gap spent working on other projects. Publishing decisions are often driven by economies of scale, and books that aren't feasible to a larger publishing house are increasingly profitable for smaller publisher or self-publishers utilising eBooks, print on demand, and crowdfunding. Notably, these shifts alter a core assumption around the way the narration time of the series: writers are increasingly sure their series can be finished, even if their initial publisher declines to take on later instalments.

It is not just economies of scale that create instability in the series. Individual narratives may be written in response to the author's cultural and historical context at the time of writing, but an ongoing series can harken back to creative or cultural trends that now feel out of date. When discussing his long-running Laundry Files series, Charlie Stross notes the ways in which his intent for the series changed in response to a shifting cultural landscape:

As of March 2019 I had been writing the Laundry Files for 20 years. Bob and the other protagonists have aged about 18 years in that time, and the world around them has changed enormously. Spies in 2019 do not mean what they meant in 1999. The political landscape in 2019 is different, and not in a good way, from 1999. "The Delirium Brief" and "The Labyrinth Index" attempted to keep the Laundry Files relevant, but it's a losing game. I really need to end the Laundry Files: I think they've got at most two books left to run.

Stross's series is produced under a traditional publishing workflow, with releases spaced twelve months or more apart, often subject to other creative and personal demands of the author and publisher involved. If we accept Marie-Laure Ryan's framing of storyworlds as a cognitive, rather than linguistic, construct that emerges after the act of reading, the importance of temporality on a series becomes obvious: a series which can be read in rapid succession builds on more recent cognitive artefacts and requires less effort to remember what came before. When indie and traditional publishers accelerate their production of series work, intentionally aiming for the season model or attempting to capture binge readers, they are also condensing the historical context in which the work is produced and read in ways that impact upon both the creative process and reader response. By pulling the release schedule into the book's field of significance, the pace of release has a corresponding productive effect on the way the books are read, the interpretive communities which form around them, and the complexity of the cognitive artefact each reader builds and brings to the next work.

The co-option of television terminology to describe series fiction is a recognition that the narration time of the series is evolving in both speed and the reliable publication of all series texts. Just as Mittell sees a transition in the poetics of the television series once it is freed from the constraints of a regularly scheduled time slot, series fiction is changed by the assumption stories will be released and accessible to all readers. Historically, the assumptions around narration time are predicated on slow production times and limited access to prior works due industry realities, including limited bookshelf space at vendors and warehouse storage. Readers in genres where series are common have long recognised the instability of long gaps between volumes. The co-option of television language to describe fiction series produced in the current marketplace is a recognition of the way the narration time around fiction has shifted, connoting a move towards regular weekly or rapid releases, eventual packaging in "boxed sets" and omnibus editions, and ready availability of backlist titles in eBook or online stories. A writer determined to continue or finish a series can do so, providing they will work outside established mainstream publishing paradigms.

The co-option of language from the sphere by authors such as Truant and Platt, as well as publishers like Serial Box, is not just a marketing term, but a promise regarding narration time and the associated management of reader memory regarding discourse time. Mittell's assertion that narration time in fiction has always been variable and allowed ready access to reading overlooks the role that narration time plays in the management of reader memory, and the assumptions and norms that emerge regarding the series. A text positioned as part of a season—particularly in the age of 'Complex TV'—is an overt acknowledgement of the interconnected nature of the text and an encouragement to binge read and make a connection between instalments in a way that has rarely been done in the history of publishing.

These expectations can have a productive effect, in addition to their marketing rhetoric. When book critic Constance Grady wrote the first Serial Box release, *Bookburners*, she noted "I put the book down in a state of profound confusion" and she "couldn't make heads or tails of the structure." (Grady) She noted this failing had nothing to do with the individual stories, which followed a conventional three-act structure and had firm endings, but the pace of revelations and twists. The series possessed an overt through line, but "there was a twist towards the end that arrived earlier than it would have in a traditional novel." (Grady) The effect was a disruption in the narrative flow, a disruption made more significant given Grady's attempt to engage with the text as a vacation read. As she notes, "I couldn't lie on the beach and lose myself in it because it actively did not want me to do so." It was not until Grady sought additional information about the series, and learned of their focus on bringing television structures to fiction, that the pacing and rhythms of *Bookburners* made sense. While it's notable that Grady read the collected edition of *Bookburners'* first season, making it easy to assume traditional book structures are in play, the collected edition offers overt clues to its structural affiliations by listing sixteen "episodes" and it's "Collected First Season" title. Going by her response, these clues were not enough to reshape Grady's expectations regarding narrative norms.

This dissonance may be at its most overt in structures that knowingly mimic the narrative norms of television, but I have encountered them in other fiction series where the demands of the series can overshadow the current story. In the prologue of Seanan McGuire's *Rosemary and Rue* (1-12), the first instalment of her *October Daye* series, her titular fey investigator has a phone conversation about her half-mortal daughter with her husband as she stakes out a fey kidnapper named Simon Torquil in 1995. McGuire does a masterful job of establishing engaging conflicts in the space of twelve pages, establishing the challenges in October Daye's life. The prologue opens with a ringing phone – the domestic, mortal world intruding on the fey, professional world of her stake-out – and while the intrusion is inconvenient, it is not unwelcome. The prologue establishes the ways Daye attempts to keep her husband from learning about her fey heritage, Daye's connection with Cliff and their daughter Gilly, Daye's near immortality compared to her mortal family, and the challenges of chasing or? tailing a subject who can use magic to hide their presence. It is a masterful set-up that establishes classic, conflicting desires within the genre: balancing the heart's desires against obligation and duty; the pleasures of present love being weighed against the pain of eternal life; the domestic challenge of wanting to be honest with your partner, but needing to hide things from them lest they be put in danger.

As the prologue progresses, McGuire sets the domestic aside and focuses on Daye's professional life as she tails Torquil to a meeting with co-conspirators. The prologue continues to establish conflicts and set reader expectations, establishing a basic knowledge of fey politics in the San Francisco setting, the political courts of light and dark fey and the respective threats they represent, and the protagonist's own position within that political landscape as a Knight of a local fey duke. The chapter escalates to a professional triumph for the protagonist, which is promptly undercut when October Daye is caught, transformed into a koi, and dropped into a pond where she spends the next fourteen years before the spell is broken. The discourse time of the novel then skips a decade of story time, during which Daye is trapped in fish form and little of narrative note occurs. When the discourse time of the narrative resumes in the first chapter, Daye is freed of her magical curse and reintegrating into the world of mortals and fey, but doing her best to keep her return a secret from the husband and daughter who have long assumed her dead and possess no knowledge of her magical nature.

As I writer, I admired the craft in that set-up. The prologue presented an engaging story question which drew me into the narrative, keenly interested in how Daye managed the reintegration of her mortal and fey lives. This was not, however, the narrative focus of *Rosemary and Rue*, which focused more on supernatural threats and Daye's attempt to reintegrate with the fey half of her dual life. While entertained, I remained frustrated that an intriguing character conflict had been drawn into the field of significance, yet not delivered upon in the story. Nor would this conflict be re-engaged with as anything more than a subplot for several more books. The prologue had been deemed necessary as set-up for the interests of the *October Daye* series, but did not serve the immediate story as well as it should. The events of the prologue informed Daye's character and needed to be known, but were not central to the first novel's story.

Admittedly, part of my confusion as a reader stemmed from the sheer weight the prologue assumed in the story. The raw page count devoted to a character or sublot within the discourse time of the story is often a way of drawing that element into a story's field of significance, foregrounding it as an element central to the good faith reading of the text. Had it been shorter, or less significant, my distemper at its disappearance might have eased considerably faster. After all, my frustration dissipated once I moved past the first book, when it was clear that the narrative threads around Day and her human family were not the primary focus. Stories teach us how to read them by establishing norms and significant elements—Mittell contends television pilots are both educational and inspiration, teaching us how to watch the show while inciting the desire to keep watching (56), and the first text within a fiction series is no different. They establish the norms and horizon of expectations which inform our reading of subsequent works, even if those norms and expectations are reshaped over time.

I suggest that the series goals lay at odd with the narrative arc of *Rosemary and Rue*. The process of orientation with regards to Day's character and long-term development across the series draw a larger subplot into the field of significance at a point where many reasons are mapping their expectations with regards to form, genre, and narrative arc. This opens two important narrative questions for series authors: how much of the discourse time can be devoted to series norms for readers unfamiliar with other works, and how can they be used to generate effects beyond recapping and managing reader memory.

Charlie Huston faces a similar challenge to McGuire in his 2006 novel *A Dangerous Man*, where his protagonist Henry Thompson is engaged in a narrative that is informed by his appearance in two prior works but is not beholden to them. Like McGuire, whose protagonist's behaviour is informed by a traumatic history, that history is not at the heart of the current story. However, Huston sidesteps the issues by positioning his recap of prior events after an opening sequence in which Henry Thompson commits murder for a Russian crime boss. Further, Huston switches to a second-person mode of narration, creating a sense of difference and distance from the immediate events of the text. What is intriguing about Huston's approach is how this switch is used to productive effect: in using second-person after starting the book in first, the narrator creates a sense of distance between the man he is in the current narrative and the man he used to be. Rather than simply orienting the reader within the series chronology, the "you" being referred to is identifiably the books narrator, Henry Thompson, using the conventions of second person narration in order to create emotional distance between his present and his past. In doing so, the recap serves a practical purpose within series poetics in addition to informing the reader about the emotional conflicts at work in the current text. While the current story of *Rosemary and Rue* is subservient to the demands of Daye's backstory and future arcs in the way she deploys discourse time, Huston uses the second person mode to both orient the reader and signpost the narrator's emotional state in a way that enhances the current story. He also devotes considerably less discourse time to the recap in terms of page count.

While a writer has little control over the narration time of their work, given the vagaries of reading speed and access to future books, the rise of the prose series built around television terminology suggests that an ideal approach is being foregrounded as part of the field of significance. Much as a streaming service like Netflix can design a TV series with binge-watching in mind, these emergent series formats foreground the assumption that works are ideally "binge read" or followed in close proximity. This is a marketing choice, but in utilising it writers and publishers are making strategic decisions that will impact on the poetics of their work.

For example, while it could be argued that Huston's approach in *A Dangerous Man* makes for a more successful book than McGuire's prologue in *Rosemary in Rue*, Huston's approach also puts the focus on the book as a stand-alone experience. The stylistic choices separate the recap from the dominant voice of the book, engaging a new regime of verisimilitude that allowing the reader to identify the change in the book's norms. In doing so, he signals to the reader that additional Henry Thompson narratives are out there, with the possibility of enhancing the reading of the current novel, but they are not required to fully comprehend and enjoy the current narrative. McGuire signposts the importance of the narratives that occur after *Rosemary and Rue*. For all the pleasures of the current novel, you are only receiving a pay-off for part of the story introduced in the prologue. Additional stories—and end-points—exist on the far side of the ellipsis when you reach the final page, with ongoing meta plots and long-term arcs that thrum beneath the respective plots of each novel. The focus still lies on providing a satisfying and successful novel, but a reader who progresses forward is promised a more fulfilling experience than the single book can provide.

In contrast, the seasonal approach utilised by Serial Box, Truant and Platt, and other indie authors take this to another extreme. Individual endings are merely stepping stones to the overall seasonal arc. The arc is a book may satisfy, but the fulfilment of the story lies at the end of the season rather than individual instalments, and series itself is the full reading experience.

To look at seriality outside of the publishing contexts that make it possible is to overlook the forces that shape poetics. While Mittell argues, correctly, that fiction is not governed by the same codified rules regarding consumption that film and television has (26), he overlooks the fact that the context of publishing have established norms and conventions regarding seriality that allow it to play to the strengths of a particular period. The narration time required to consume a novel or story may be variable, but the shifting norms in terms of access and release have triggered an evolution in fiction seriality, and writers are responding in kind.

While many of the writers challenging the norms of series publishing have emerged from field of self-publishing, they are not alone in seeing the potential these shifts hold in writing a successful series narrative. Fantasy fiction—a genre once dominated by the trilogy as a series form – is increasingly embracing narratives that flout that norm. Indeed, some authors steeped in traditional publishing practices are eagerly embracing the shift. In an interview with Joanna Penn, sci-fi and fantasy author Kevin J Anderson discussed the difficulties with switching his focus from epic science fiction and fantasy stories to a more horror-based detective series. In particular, he notes the challenge in finding a balance between industry expectations and the norms established by successful series within his particular subgenre. At the time he conceived of the series, Anderson was already a successful author, noting his track record with "23 million books in print". Despite this, his usual publishers were reluctant to take a chance on a book outside his usual genres of epic fantasy and science fiction. Once he placed the series with a smaller publisher, Anderson "wrote all three books so they could bring them out very, very swiftly". The results were not a commercial success, and the contract was cancelled after the second book was released.

This flew in the face of Anderson's own understanding of what it took to make a series a success, particularly in the dark fantasy detective space he was moving into. He notes:

> *I contacted some of my other friends who wrote series like that, Jim Butcher, and Kelly Armstrong, and Patricia Briggs, and Sherrilyn Kenyon. And every one of them told me that it took at least six books before their series took off. My publisher published the first two those Dan Shamble books and said, "It's not taking off so we're just gonna finish this up. (Anderson)*

When the rights reverted, Anderson published the books with Wordfire, the small publishing house he co-owns and runs with his spouse Rebecca Moesta. At the time of the interview in 2016, Anderson noted his intent to write another volume, and cited the success of the books under his own imprint, noting that "I'm actually making more money now from my own publishing efforts than what they did" (Anderson). Intriguingly, checking in on the series three years later, it now sits at the full six instalments recommended to him by Butcher, Armstrong, Briggs, and Kenyon.

Part of Anderson's decisions to self-publish is driven by his knowledge that traditional publishing's expectations are not supportive of the long series, noting that "it used to be a publishing would invest in Jim Butcher and they would stick with his series for six books" in the hopes of success, but now series work is likely to be cut if it doesn't skyrocket immediately. Obviously, economies of scale are in play here. The number of copies a self-published author needs to sell in order to find a return on their investment is considerably lower than the number of copies an established publishing house must sell in order to receive a return on their investment. What is notable, however, is the impact this has on series poetics. In Complex TV, Mittell notes that a precursor for storytelling innovations in the television space was "the recalibrations of industry expectations for what a hit series looked like" (34). As with Anderson's novel, the overall size of the audience is measured against the expectations of the publisher.

Anderson's situation raises two intriguing questions. First, what constitutes success in a series? Second, does the length of a series hold significance for its reception and success? The potential pleasures and poetic possibilities inherent in the long-format series are frequently complicated by the volatile relationship series fiction has with the publishing industry, going through periods where series formats fall in and out of vogue. Recurring characters that appealed to readers were an asset in the wood pulp era. For example, Erle Stanley Gardner produced 49 series characters over his career, and maintained 13 series characters simultaneously in 1934 alone, publishing twenty-eight novelettes and three series novels besides his stand-alone work (Fugate & Fugate ch. 10)—all notably before the creation of his most iconic series creation, Perry Mason. More recently, editor and author Kristine Kathryn spent a 2011 blog post discussing the appeal of digital publishing to genre authors, noted the cycle of attitudes she's seen regarding series works across her long career as a writer, editor, and publisher:

> *Then there were the series that I had to abandon because of the changes in publishing. In the 1980s and early 1990s, book publishers loved series. More than that, they loved poaching series from another publisher. Publisher A couldn't make your series work? Publisher B was happy to snatch up the next book*

> —mid-series—and prove to Publisher A how stupid their marketing department was.
>
> But with the collapse of the distribution system in the late 1990s, the consolidation of publishing houses, and the layoff of countless employees, suddenly this poaching practice stopped. A series wasn't doing as well as it could for Publisher A? Well, then no other publisher would touch it. A series was doing passably well for Publisher A? Then no other publisher would want it mid-book, because they'd have to grow the series—and that wasn't a guaranteed bestseller. (Rusch)

Rusch then advocates for the return of the series in the digital publishing space, and she is not alone in that. High-profile self-publishing advocates such as Mark Dawson, Joanna Penn, and Dean Wesley Smith all advocate for the creation of series as a publishing strategy, arguing that a publisher need only capture a reader's attention with a new work once, then sell them on the familiarity of an ongoing series. Serial works, it seems, are gaining ground as a tactic utilised by genre authors in the contemporary publishing landscape, although the logic of these choices is usually driven by commercial concerns as much as literary aesthetics.

Early advocates for independent publishing using digital tools were quick to hail the technology as the second coming of the pulp fiction era, with veteran writer, editor, and commentator Dean Wesley Smith arguing "Indie publishing favours prolific writers, just as the pulp era did." Certainly, the popular take-up of eBooks and the self-published business model led to an increased amount of online rhetoric about writing fast. In 2011, fantasy author Rachel Aaron's blog post "How I Went From Writing 2,000 Words a Day to 10,000 Words a Day" attracted viral attention, and soon spawned a book detailing her methodology. Additional advocates for increased writing speed soon followed, including Chris Fox's *5,000 Words Per Hour: Write Faster, Write Smarter*, while thriller author Russel Blake received mainstream coverage in the Wall Street Journal in 2014 after producing 25 books in 30 months to take advantage of Amazon's new release algorithms as a marketing tactic (Alter). What these authors share with Platt and Truant, mentioned at the start of this chapter, is an interest in fusing an aggressive release schedule with the use of series works to hold the reader's attention. The rhetoric around rapid production eventually solidified into the production strategy dubbed 'rapid release' in independent publishing circles, and emerging writers incapable of matching the aggressive production speed are advised to stockpile books in order to take advantage of the compressed reading time between books.

It's easy to observe this production rhetoric and see the concerns of those who fear the subject of popular fiction—and self-published popular fiction at that—a disrespectable subject for a research-driven higher degree. If we take Bourdieu's assertion that art can be created for its own sake, or done for the sake of the market, self-publishing's interest in manipulating the reading time of a series is all too often an economic choice. Indeed, one of the largest online Facebook groups for writers interested in independent publishing, 20 Books to 50K, connects economic success with the rapid production of books ("What's with…"). While Bourdieu's binary stretches a long shadow across the literary field, my lived experience as a writer suggests the binary is more akin to a spectrum. As Kim Wilkins notes, contemporary writers "have to make our peace with the tension between the demands of art and the demands of commerce" ("Do the hustle"). Any writer who seeks an audience will be in negotiation with the marketplace, and so the commercial forces shape our practice while also being shaped by them.

My ultimate decision to bring self-published works into my engagement ultimately came down to three decisions. First, my writing practice positions me as a 'hybrid' author, with my creative output split between small press publications and self-published works. In contrast to Bourdieu's binary, it is frequently my more commercial works that find traditional publication, while my more experimental or artistically driven works are brought out under my publishing imprint.

Second, I believe the commercial choices made by many self-published authors open intriguing poetic possibilities, not least because they are freed from commercial constraints. As Mitel notes, Complex TV did not just emerge because of technological shifts, but because technological shifts prompted "the recalibration of industry expectations for what a hit series looked like" (34). Similarly, the reduced overheads and economies of scale associated with digital publishing allow authors to 'succeed' with series works that would be deemed economically unviable by a traditional publisher, opening up the possibility of intriguing experimentation or representations. Independent works may lend themselves to popular genres, but they are not necessarily a mass market phenomenon. In this environment, series end on the authors' terms rather than a publisher's disinclination to produce additional works.

Finally, advocates who embrace the notion of digital publishing's growth in self-publishing and small press as a new or neo-pulp environment often underestimate the fundamental point of difference between the current landscape and the magazine or paperback era in which pulp writers operated and highly commercial, 'generic' genre works reigned supreme. Both the terminology and framing of the divide between 'indie-publishing', 'self-publishing' and 'traditional publishing' give preference to those who use the publishing model, rather than the publishing model itself. In 2013, Kristine Kathryn Rusch proposed an alternate take on the two business models, suggesting traditional publishing may be better thought of as Velocity Publishing, while indie publishing has embraced back-list driven marketing. For Rusch, velocity publishers "measure everything by sales velocity—how many copies the book sells *quickly*" ("Discovery..."), often coupled with heavy promotion to drive attention before the book is released. Meanwhile, backlist-driven publishing has watched the rise of backlist sales since 2010 with interest, and no longer creates meaningful divisions between their front list and backlist titles when promoting published works.

Proponents of the "new pulp" era overlook the importance of velocity and scarcity that drove the sales of pulp fiction. Pulp magazines proved a temporary format, published on degradable, low-quality paper with a comparatively short shelf-life. Even the pulp paperback market, which emerged after the magazines folded, built its marketing strategies around the assumption books would sell for a limited of time, each release quickly replaced on store shelves and racks, because the cost to warehouse back list titles frequently outstrip the potential profit. Books sold in eBook or print on demand formats are not subject to such limitations. Indeed, they are typically only removed from sale at the author's request. In such an environment, every work a writer produces—in theory, and often practice—is available for as long as there are folks willing to host the files and profit from it.

While the earliest days of eBooks were driven by a ferocious need for content, the glut of new works in competition with easily accessible backlists creates an environment where innovation and artistic merit can be an intriguing market differentiator within a particular genre field. Series fiction that might be dubbed a failure under the velocity publishing model can find success as their backlist grows, especially given the pleasures of seriality may not reveal themselves until several narratives exist.

It has in this spirit that I have approached the Dana Valkyrie novellas, with the goal of producing five distinct stories designed to leverage the backlist-driven publishing model. Their serial aspects are intentionally drawn into the field of significance: first, by the release as individual works, but also via meta-textual elements and subtitles that reinforce the elliptical nature of the series even when collected as a single volume. As I will discuss in the next chapter, these five stories will be framed as a single season, intentionally ending with a change in the status quo and suggesting future stories. They are written with the goal of releasing the series rapidly—one novella every three months—making creative choices with the reader who consumes the series quickly in mind.

However, these stories also exist as part of a creative writing thesis, and issues of series temporality present challenges with the context of thesis submission. There are obvious constraints are placed on creative projects, as laid out by the University of Queensland website, which posits submissions should:

> *Display originality, a critical understanding of genre, and make a significant contribution to the practice. It typically takes the form of (1) a work of prose of approximately 60,000 words; or (2) a poetry manuscript of approximately 96 pages; or (3) a screenplay for a feature film; a script for a number of episodes of a television series or full-length theatre production; or a script for radio production or any other medium as approved by the advisory team. ("Creative writing PhD thesis format")*

I invested considerable debate in how best to explore the temporal aspects of seriality within these constraints. Early consideration was given to producing a short story collection of multiple stories or novelettes, but I discarded this option after considering the ways collecting the work as a single whole might impact the narration time associated with consuming the work. While series texts may be written and read against the expectation of the series, their seriality sits alongside expectations of the individual text's narrative format, genre, culture of production, and many others. I believe, as David Jauss argues, that while a story is a discrete text, the act of sequencing a collection allows for connections and disruptions as the texts are read against one another (150-151). Both collections and series draw the connections between texts into the field of significance, but the act of collection "creates an elaborate system of parallels, contrasts, repetitions, and variations that creates unity out of diversity" (151). The collection becomes a singular reading experience, even if its comprised of unrelated texts. In short, we expect different things from a collection than we do a series, even if they share complimentary goals. Further, because collections are often comprised of shorter works, the choice to write novellas is a strategic choice to disrupt expectations. While a collection of short stories may be published as a singular whole, conventions suggest longer works are more likely to see publication as stand-alone titles, and even when collected together, their length pulls seriality into the zone of significance.

To further combat this tendency to view the series as a collection, I have presented two of the novellas produced for the series, representing works at the beginning and the end of the five-volume sequence. Both works are clearly marked by subtitle and presented as "bookends" to this critical work, creating a divide in the proposed reading experience. While readers are under no obligation to follow this proposed order, the positioning itself serves to reinforce the 'polite' way to read the works and invoke a horizon of expectations congruent with series poetics, even if the other volumes are not available.

The challenge of this submission strategy lay in creating two series texts that were satisfying and coherent for the reader without access to the three texts not included in this submission. This required an embrace of the successive series format, informed by my growing awareness of strategies and techniques employed by authors of such series. For a writer steeped in years of producing stories built around character chance and dramatic arcs, it also demanded a new understanding of how characters might be rendered and made engaging to the reader over multiple texts. In the next chapter, I will interrogate the possibilities inherent in serial characterisation, and the ways they often fly in the face of received wisdom around character development and story craft.

NAVIGATING THE ELLIPSIS
STORY, CHARACTER, AND ENDINGS IN SERIES WORKS

Academic language surrounding literature does not always capture the experiential knowledge of writers, particularly when applied to foundational ideas that get passed on through writing guides, workshops, mentorships, and other developmental opportunities that target practitioners as they develop. Even these attempts to convey techniques around plot and structure struggle with a divide identified by Samuel Delany (2005): the term plot "refers to an affect the story produces in the *reading*. But writing is an internal process writers go through (or put themselves through) in front of a blank page that leaves the detritus of words there" (69). And yet, Delany is also aware of the critical role that reading and criticism play in a writer's development, allowing the writer to absorb complex models for the sentence, the narrative scene, and larger literary structures (119). As countless writers are informed as they start their careers, thou must read before you can write.

The challenge, Delany argues, is submitting to those internalised models (119) and adjusting it to the project at hand. He argues that "there's very little creativity in creativity. The vast majority is submission—submission to the laws of grammar, to the possibilities of rhetoric, to the grammar of narrative, to narrative's various and possible structurings" (121). For a writer used to submitting to the narrative grammar of the standalone novel or short story, writing series work has the potential to introduce a disruptive element to the creative process that's deceptive in its simplicity: this story must resolve, but the narrative proceeds. Individual narrative endings are not a full stop, but an ellipsis promising more to come if and when the series resumes. In this chapter, I will explore the impact these ellipsis have on the reading experience, along with the creative opportunities they open up to generate new and series-specific effects.

There are countless attempts to chart the grammar of narrative for aspiring writers, and the transformative journey of the protagonist lies at the heart of many. A brief perusal of popular writing guides from James Scott Bell, Christopher Vogler, and Blake Snyder present structural models for story that echo the transformative hero's journey laid out in Joseph Campbell's *Hero with a Thousand Faces*, many of them aimed at aspiring novelists, short fictioneers, and screenwriters. For many such guides, the notion that a character must change internally is a vital component of telling a successful story: in *The Anatomy of Story*, John Truby argues that character change "is what gives the audience the deepest satisfaction" (32), with the climax of the narrative highlighting said change through the moral choice made by the protagonist (35); and in her book, *Story Genius*, Lisa Cron argues that "a story is about how the things that happen affect someone in pursuit of a difficult goal, and how that person changes internally as a result" (8). In discussing the short story, James Scott Bell argues we predicate the form upon the fallout of a single shattering moment in the protagonist's lives (*How to Write* Ch 3), that changes everything together. Across all the guides is a recurring focus on the protagonists change across the story, and the need for a character arc is instilled in many writers as part of their early development. To use a constant refrain in writing workshops: your protagonist is the character with the most to lose, about to undergo the most significant change.

This perspective suggests an understanding of a character's internal state and progression towards a better self is central to the craft of telling a story, even if they ultimately choose not to change. Blakey Vermuele argues the understanding of a character's interiority can be vital to our enjoyment of fiction. Our assumption of our character's personhood is related to a psychological assumption of agency: "We see something propelling itself, something directing itself towards a goal, and we think it has a self, that it has intentions" (23). Similarly, "people are uniquely fascinated by events that disturb their innate dualism," (26) a state that is frequently exploited by narrative advice to establish both external, physical challenges and internal, moral conflicts for narrative protagonists. For a species with a high preference for social information, this access to another's interiority holds a powerful appeal. The challenge of series fiction lies in its prolonged access to a character's interior state, with a subsequent need for consistency of both desires, self-awareness, and memory of prior events.

One method of managing this need for consistency in series fiction is use of an iconic protagonist, a term coined by editor Robin Laws in the introduction to his 2012 anthology, *The New Hero*. Here, Laws noted the challenge he presented to his contributors—to create an iconic hero, stepping away from the transformative narratives that dominate the way we talk about character and story (7-8). Rather than narratives where the protagonist is psychologically or morally changed, Laws sought out stories where the conflict presented a challenge to the hero's ethos, which was subsequently resolved when the protagonist used their skills and innate ethical surety to return the narrative world to a state of order (6). In doing this, he advocated a small, but vital, change to popular conceptions of narrative: while the dramatic hero resolves the disorder in their world via an act of internal transformation, the iconic hero resolves the disorder in theirs by cleaving to their essential self.

Laws use of ethos in this context harkens back to Aristotles poetics, and the imitation of men either "either as better than in real life, or as worse, or as they are" (2), and in which narrative action is designed to reveal moral purpose (8). When identifying nine exemplar iconic heroes in popular culture, Laws draws a strong correlation between the iconic and the tendency to enhance a character's merits and flaws. Intriguingly, all his examples are closely associated with serial forms. Although some are drawn from the medium of television (Gregory House from the television series *House*), it also includes a series of characters who have their origins in fiction novels and short stories, among them James Bond, Miss Marple, Sherlock Holmes, Conan the Barbarian, and Tarzan. The iconic and the series is immediately connected and drawn in stark contrast to the typical dramatic arc that dominates contemporary narratives.

This choice is no coincidence: in his subsequent book on writing, *Beating the Story*, Laws specifically calls out the iconic hero as a character archetype built with series in mind. He believes that their procedurally-driven conflicts, and their return to philosophical certainty, ensures these heroes are capable of reiterating their conflicts over multiple, unrelated adventures (ch. 1). The iconic hero's narrative serves to tests their inner moral compass and their external abilities, but the resolution is dependent on the iconic hero's abilities being used to reiterate their internal ethos and return to a place of certitude (ch. 1). This shifts the focus of the series towards recurring affirmation of the character, rather than progressive transformation, and even in genres where successive and dramatic are the norm—such as romance—the repeated affirmation of a core ideal provides the unifying theme.

The iconic hero suggests two lines of interrogation for writers of series: first, it invites us to consider how series narratives may differ from a stand-alone text; second, how can these differences be used to achieve poetic effects beyond the singular story? The moral competence of the iconic protagonist often stems from a source of internal conflict, the same unspoken psychic wound or void that powers the arc of their dramatic cousins. Such protagonists are still driven by the desire to have their wound resolved, but their iconic narratives drive towards temporary, often metaphorical, resolutions: Jack Reacher can never belong in the civilised America he travels through; Bruce Wayne can never save his parents, no matter how many criminals he defeats; Sherlock Holmes will never find stimulus to sufficiently engage his incredible mind. The stories in which they feature represents temporary diversions, a momentary respite from the pain of the psychic wound.

This may strike some as an attempt to draw too fine a line between the two archetypes, especially with regards to narrative structure. Both iconic and dramatic characters are driven by internal discontent and experience a disruption in the status quo at the beginning of the narrative. The dramatic hero takes this disruption as a spur to evolve and change, while the iconic hero sublimates their desire, effectively rendering themselves a tragic figure. Yet this fine line provides a useful lens for understanding the appeal of the iconic hero over a series. The writing of an iconic series hero relies not on the progression of a story across the life of a series, but in finding sufficient variations and challenges to the iconic ethos to present a new and engaging reading experience, allowing us to experience their interiority in different contexts.

More importantly, Laws distillation of the iconic hero also provides a useful filter for examining successive series that don't rely on a recurring iconic hero. A romance series such as Lauren Dane's *Brown Family* novels often utilises a dramatic structure, with the hero and heroine drawn together and fundamentally changed by the events of the novel. However, each new novel presents a different pairing drawn from secondary characters from earlier works. The novels are not progressive but offer a similar variation on an iconic motif and dramatic arc, in this case the power of love and acceptance as an aid to processing and moving past trauma. Readers may be presented with different protagonists in each new novel but retain the comforting challenge to the core ethos and resolving of that challenge in each new novel.

These repetitions make iconic characters frequent targets for detractors of genre fiction, who point to the repetition and lack of dramatic growth as hallmarks of popular writing. To argue the quality of these stories is, perhaps, the least interesting aspect of them. Rather than shut down our engagement, I am more intrigued by the opportunities these repetitions open up to canny writers of series. Just as conventions of meter and rhyme can push a poet to find new modes of expression, recurring conventions can be used by writers of series fiction to create poetic effects beyond the structural guidelines of their craft.

However, such attempts are likely hindered by our lack of real understanding of series models. While a writer may play to or against genre conventions, as Gaiman suggests, the ability to do so is predicated on a shared understanding those conventions exist between the writer and the broader interpretive community.

The narratives of iconic heroes serve to test both their inner compass and their external abilities, but the final resolution is dependent on the iconic hero's abilities being used to reiterate their internal ethos and return to a place of certitude (Laws, ch. 1). This shifts the focus of the series towards recurring affirmation of the character, rather than progressive transformation.

It may be tempting to conflate Laws' iconic hero with the successive model of seriality proposed by Victor Watson, treating them as two articulations of the same series structure. This suggests a similarly natural correlation between the dramatic arcs Laws contrasts the dramatic hero against and the successive narrative mode. I argue series poetics are far more nuanced, as series works need to be successful as individual works and as part of the larger series structure.

The series author invites the reader to progress by bringing the seriality of the text into the field of significance, but the reader will only do so if the individual texts satisfy. In *Writing the Fiction Series* (2013), Karen Wiesner dubs this the divide between story arc and series arc. The story arc is specific to a particular book (ch. 2), while "an overall series arc is a plot thread that's introduced in the first book in the series, is alluded to in some way in every subsequent book but is only fully resolved in the final book of the series" (ch. 2). These series arcs play out separately to the story arc, effectively running beneath the story arc of the individual works (ch. 2) although some series eschew the series arc in favour of being more open-ended (ch. 2). In doing so, Wiesner identifies the same divide between progressive and successive series models identified by Victor Watson, although she frames the distinction by the way in which narrative behaves. However, Wiesner's framing also opens up the possibility that these distinctions operate as a spectrum, as a progressive element in a series may be a focal point of an individual entry's plot, a subplot, or a momentary allusion, depending on the text. Within this framing an iconic character may allude to an ongoing dramatic arc, even if it's never truly resolved.

It's here, once again, turning towards the field of television studies offers some useful insight in terms of series poetics. Central to the development of the television poetics Mittell has dubbed Complex TV is the changing role of characterisation within the television format. With the introduction of DVD technology, and increased consumer access to episodes that can be re-watched and studied, creators embraced the opportunity for "extended character depth, ongoing plotting, and episodic variations" (32) that would be impossible in a two-hour film narrative. These narratives would have been impossible to create in the pre-DVD era due to the episodic constraints, a risk-adverse industry, and a viewing experience that demands consumers engage with the work on a specific schedule. Notably, Mittell sees the biggest limitation of this pre-DVD era in narrative terms: "most successful television series typically lack the crucial element that has long been hailed as of supreme importance for a well-told story: an ending" (33). As a medium television embraced a successive series model and its infinite, iterative freedom to continue so long as ratings held and advertisers were interested.

This model frequently demanded iconic character and minimal progression, leading to protagonists who reverted to form at the end of every episode and rarely recalled the events of one episode in subsequent narratives. The move away from this mode of storytelling saw the introduction of seasonal arcs and highly narrative, progressive works such as *The Wire* in which each episode is a step in an ongoing, highly connected season-long story. These series grant us long-term access to characters and their interiority, but still play by the conventions of the form. As Mittell notes, "While it may seem that a pleasure of serial narratives is watching characters grow and develop over time, most television characters are more stable and consistent rather than changeable entities" (133). The appeal of the successive series still lies in the repetition of familiar elements and repeated exposure to the interiority of an evolving, progressing character. To change a character is to introduce an instability to each successive story—one that must be reconciled by making each change momentary or irrelevant, and therefore less satisfying, or through introducing progressive elements such as chronology and a specific order of narrative consumption that makes the character's evolution comprehensible.

Rather than focusing on character change as an end-point, Mittell argues it is one of multiple possibilities that might satisfy the reader. In doing so, he invokes the work of two critics who concern themselves with how and why we respond to fictional characters, Blakey Vermule and the film theorist Murray Smith. While many writing guides frame empathy as central to identifying with a character, both Smith and Vermule seek a more nuanced explanation for why we are drawn to and invest in characters. Writers may be fond of the conceit that characters come to life in the process of writing, but ultimately characters are artificial constructs: "no more than collections of inert, textually described traits" which we assume "correspond to analogical ones we find in persons in the real world, unless this is explicitly contradicted by a description in the text" (Vermule 82). For Smith, empathic identification is one part of a complex whole, arguing that such engagement is born of three more precise concepts: recognition, alignment, and allegiance on the part of the reader (73). While engaging with fiction is an imaginative activity, it is both mediated and constrained by the act of narration that presents causal links between events (74). Significantly, for writers of series, Smith also identifies the recurrence and re-identification of a character as a narrative marker for character complexity.

This seems an intuitive point for many writers, but it underscores a significant narrative process. For Smith, re-identification establishes continuity of the character, "allowing us to say that a certain figure is continuous with a figure apprehended at an earlier or later point in the narrative, by virtue of certain bonds of similarity and causality" (113). This, in turn, allows audiences to recognise and discriminate between degrees of complexity, stereotypicality, plausibility, artificiality, attachment, and subjective transparency when regarding characters presented in a text (116). The invocation of causality evokes the spectre of E. M. Forster's distinction between flat and round characters, but as Smith notes, this reduces a complex field down to a simple oppositional binary (116). Within the context of series works, the notion of recurrence takes on new dimensions, as seemingly minor characters can recur in multiple works and accrete an ongoing causality across the breadth of the series.

I argue this attachment can be deployed for poetic effect, even in the absence of overt dramatic arcs, as reader alignment and allegiance are two functions which are normally invoked in discussion of character empathy. Notably, Smith separates identifying the importance of a character from the process of *alignment*, or "the process by which spectators are placed in relation to characters in terms of access to their actions, and what they know and feel" (83). For Smith, alignment governs our sense of connection with a character, mediated by the level of attachment the reader is allowed via the space they occupy in the narrative and the amount of subjective access the reader has to their interior states (142). Moreover, once a reader has recognised a character and been placed in alignment with them, the recognition of new characters is subjected to mediation produced by the existing character alignments (144). For writers of prose, rather than film, these processes are mediated not just by choices around point of view and the use of first, second, or third person narrators, but also by the amount of narration time devoted to a character on the page.

The final aspect of Smith's character model, *allegiance*, incorporates the moral evaluation of the characters by the spectator (84), integrating both emotional and cognitive responses (187). The distinction between allegiance and alignment is often demonstrated by archetypal antiheroes and other protagonists who dominate the alignment-structure of a narrative but remain unsympathetic throughout (188). This separation provides a useful lens for viewing the structural patterns of dramatic narrative, where the power of the protagonist's moral choice at the climax is also the strongest narrative invocation of the reader's allegiance as the protagonist transcends their less empathetic traits.

Building on Smith's work, Mittell notes that "attachment is a crucial variable, as our relative connection to individuals can shift from episode to episode, and nearly all serials have a pattern of multiple attachments to an ensemble of characters" (129). While Smith focuses on the deployment of character constructs in a single narrative framework, Mittell notes that a series that starts focusing strongly on a single protagonist will gradually widen its focus over several episodes (129). Every recurrence of a character increased attachment as they are identified, aligned with, and potentially allied with, allowing secondary and tertiary characters to take on greater significance in the eyes of fans. This, in turn, invites a stronger identification with setting and scenario than individual protagonists (120). The fiction series may have slightly more focus; unlike television, where an expanded cast of point-of-view characters is a practical production decision, a fiction writer is free to deploy a single POV. Even in an iconic series such as Lee Child's *Jack Reacher* novels, focused on an itinerant protagonist with a shifting supporting cast each time, the repetition of elements such as Reacher's brother and his relationship with military authorities generate the sense of expansion Mittell speaks of.

This slow development of secondary and minor characters is a powerful device for series works, and one inaccessible in a stand-alone narrative where attempts to increase engagement will require an increased focus on the character within the narrative. To appear for a single scene ever book, over ten books, is a very different framing than appearing ten times within a single narrative. Mittell foregrounds the importance these processes of attachment are for series works:

> *Attachment is particularly important for serials, as spending time with characters encourages parasocial connections — the more time we spend with particular characters, the more we extend that time through hypothetical and paratextual engagement outside the moments of watching. (130)*

Compared to a stand-alone narrative, series works offer a long-term investment, allowing the audience to accrue knowledge and experiences and posit our own version of character interiority (132). Central to this slow burn engagement with the characters is the way Smith's attachment model is experienced across a dynamic, shifting system rather than a fixed narrative (133). What is true of minor characters is also true of central, iconic protagonists, who are lent complexity born of repetition, courtesy of the reader's repeated opportunities to identify characters and align our expectations. Mittell frames this strength as character elaboration, rather than character change (136). Crucially, series narrative "exploits the serial form to gradually reveal aspects of a character over time so that these facets of the character feel new to the audience, even if they are consistent and unchanging character attributes" (136). While a static, dramatic narrative draws upon the reader's allegiances to make the choices at the climax feel meaning, an iconic character introduces those same complexities through revelation of new details or introducing new contexts that shift the reader's knowledge and framing of their actions.

Iconic heroes need not abandon the complexity of their dramatic counterparts. In Mittell's framing of character, the moral epiphanies and choices that drive dramatic narratives are best described as a character transformation, marking "a gradual shift of morality, attitudes, and sense of self that manifests itself in altered actions and long-term repercussions" (141). Progressive narratives, which often build an ongoing dramatic arc, often use the end-points of individual stories to mark significant moments in those shifts. While these kinds of transformations may occur more often in television narrative, Mittell argues for a more sophisticated vocabulary when discussing serialised characters, noting that *transformation* is very different to commonly used developments such as character *growth*, when a character becomes fleshed out over time (137); character *education*, in which individual stories or arcs key life lessons spread over time (138); and character *overhauls* in which "someone undergoes a dramatic sudden shift, often tied to a supernatural or fantastic situation that creates body switches or clones, but we retain our serial memories of earlier events and relationships" (138-139). In many of these cases, the intent is not to invoke closure, as the dramatic epiphany does, but invoke curiosity about the shift in context and its implications to the characters and world on the far side of the ellipsis.

Both Laws' iconic/dramatic model and Watson's theories of progressive and successive modes of series offer useful insights into existing series archetypes. However, I argue the two are considerably more useful when deployed as a matrix of understanding the conventions around series structures, and in particular when establishing the series norms within a particular genre. Laws' distinction between iconic and dramatic protagonists suggests how the characters are utilised within the context of an individual story, while Watson's theories speak to the relationship established between the component texts. When arrayed as complementary tools, rather than simultaneous ones, we can build a framework that clarifies series assumptions and behaviours, both in terms of the individual narratives and the importance of events happening in the ellipsis between stories.

A fantasy trilogy like *Lord of the Rings*, for example, is predicated on the assumptions of a progressive narrative epic featuring dramatic arcs. The hard-boiled detective stories of Raymond Chandler are a successive series featuring an iconic hero. A romance series, such as Lauren Dane's *Brown Family* stories, will typically feature dramatic heroes in a successive series structure. Within this frame, Laws' conception of the iconic hero provides an intriguing model for understanding how many successive series achieve their ongoing iteration—by utilising a challenge to a core ethos as a unifying feature—but does not require it of the character.

Further, this model suggests how certain series iterate without a central main character. The romance genre is dominated by series in which protagonists undergo dramatic arcs and then step aside as a central figure. For example, the first volume of Dane's *Brown Family* series, *Laid Bare*, focuses on the rekindled romantic liaisons of rockstar Erin Brown several years after she retired from public life after her daughter was killed by a stalker. Over the course of the novel, falling in love and finding support in her partner sees her agree to a short tour with her younger brother, completing a dramatic arc and showing the fundamental change expected of dramatic protagonists. The second novel, *Coming Undone*, focuses on the romantic liaisons of her elder brother Brody and a new neighbour, but features a similar focus on the power of found family and love as a catalyst for recovering from trauma in the portrayal of Brody's antagonist, Elise. This trend continues for another four novels and an accompanying novella, always shifting focus to a different family member or friend. Each novel is driven by a dramatic arc, but the series itself is successive. What unifies it is not a central character, but the recurring themes that underpin each dramatic arc.

Both Watson and Laws frame series works around two archetypes, but in combining their models we open up a more nuanced framing and understanding of series structures. If, as Pavel suggests, genre norms represent successful artistic solutions that the writer may work to or again (209), then developing a clearer framework for understanding series structures allows agents within the publishing field to better understand the artistic solutions that have come before and utilise models that best fit their goals.

When Victor Watson argues that series works are ideally suited to "effectively express the ambivalence towards age and time that is central to the experience of childhood" (7), he foregrounds the productive role series structure plays in the interpretation of series text. I argue the progressive/successive divide is one component, and that by combining it with a study of the way time and character are utilised within a particular work, we can visualise a more complex framework for understanding serial poetics and their ability to present complex characters. To explore this, I will turn away from the genres of young adult and children's fiction, and towards a branch of speculative fiction whose protagonists have their own ambivalence towards age and time: series fictions featuring vampires.

Elizabeth Bear's *New Amsterdam* stories and Cherie Priest's *Raylene Pendle* novels both present the reader with long-lived vampire heroes who cleave to gothic tropes of the isolated outsider, ostensibly using the age of the character within the story world to frame that isolation. However, decisions made regarding the use of a dramatic or iconic character archetype, series structure, and the publishing environment in which the stories are consumed conspire to provide a prospective reader with very different readings of that undead isolation.

The first book in Cherie Priest's series, *Bloodshot*, gives Raylene Pendle a dramatic arc in addition to procedural conspiracy investigation that drives the narrative forward. When Pendle first appears, she is defined by her hatred of new people (9), her separation from vampiric society (7, 27), and her desire for isolation in the name of safety. Pendle keeps her distance—physically and metaphorically—from both the young squatters that live below her and the professional colleagues she relies upon as a burglar.

Over the course of the first narrative, she undergoes a dramatic change on all fronts: falling for her client, a fellow vampire; adopting the squatters after her actions put them in danger; and establishing a regular ongoing working relationship and friendship with an ex-SEAL she encounters during the investigation. The next book sees her dramatic arc continue when she is forced to re-engage with vampiric society and confront the events of her past. This positions the *Raylene Pendle* novels as a progressive series underpinned by dramatic transformation, albeit one built around a procedural concept in which Pendle engages in acts of investigation and theft.

Meanwhile, Bear's Don Sebastian du Ulloa is a vampire detective, and his central ethical pre-occupations are outlined in his first appearance. Two, in particular, are drown into the field of significance for the reader. In the first story in the series chronology, du Ulloa notes nothing gives his undead existence a sense of satisfaction like watching a murder scrambling to avoid justice (58). Similarly, later in the story, Sebastian tries to force his young lover to leave because he knows he cannot give the young man a life together because "life is for the living, not the undead" (62). Don Sebastian is the primary protagonist for many of the stories in the *New Amsterdam* series, although he cedes this role to a second character—the forensic sorcerer Abigail Irene Garrett—in four of the early narratives. In these stories, he becomes a narrative foil for Garrett as her preoccupations drive the narrative. While their relationship develops across the length of the series, it does not drive it; the changes are not dramatic, but underscore Sebastian's belief that he is being unfair—or unjust—to the mortals that come to love him.

Effectively, Sebastian's narratives do not mark moments of change for the character, but a temporary respite from his vampiric plight. When each story begins with a case or a source of injustice, he is presented with an opportunity to focus on problems he can resolve, rather than dwelling on the ethical difficulties of his immortality.

The chronology of their respective story worlds frequently plays an important role in both vampire's narratives. Raylene Pendle and Don Sebastian have both lived through far more of the story time in their respective worlds than any of the mortals they encounter, and the motivations for both characters are contextualised by the weight those years carry within the story world. However, the readers experience of their lives is not grounded by story time, but by the events and time-periods presented in the discourse time of the story. Here, the presentations of the two vampires diverge strongly: the two volumes in the *Raylene Pendle* series occur in less than twelve months, while the stories of the *New Amsterdam* series cover 63 years, with the first story taking place in March, 1899, followed by a cluster of five stories taking place between 1901 and 1903, only to advance to 1938 and 1962 in the final two stories.

This choice frames the immortal solitude of Don Sebastian in a very crucial way, as mortal characters, including the co-protagonist, Abigail Irene Garrett, age and die over the course of the series. These changes draw impact from the switch in POV characters, giving the reader the opportunity to align with Garret as a central protagonist in earlier work, giving us greater access to her interiority than other members of the supporting cast, only to move her back into a secondary role in later texts. For readers who have allied with her, alongside Don Sebastian, the loss is palpably stronger than for those who have only encountered her in the penultimate novella.

The kinds of stories told—whether iconic or dramatic—within that story time also make a statement about what undeath means within the story world. For example, while both characters have their motivations tied to the tedium of immortality and the difficulties vampires have in changing with the times, Raylene Pendle's narratives see her internal motivations rapidly evolve across a year and make significant internal and external changes. In the first story, "New Amsterdam", Don Sebastian is still absorbed in the same ethical and activities across all 63 years of his lifespan represented in the discourse time. While Raylene evolves away from who she is in a short period, Don Sebastian is effectively trapped in a recurring conflict that shows no sign of abating. One we align with him in one story, our alignment and allegiance to him as a character is tested in new time periods and contexts. This suggests his failure to evolve or change extends beyond the discourse time covered by the series narratives, extending through a long, undead existence in a way no single story could portray.

The choices made regarding discourse time also hold three significant considerations regarding series characterisation. First, it tells us what is narratively significant within the story world; second, it tells us who is important through the number of scenes they occupy, and the points of view used to depict events; finally, the events drawn into the field of significance by the discourse time invites the reader to draw connection between the scenes and the stories that make up the discourse. While a progressive series makes the link between individual stories explicit—the events dramatised within the discourse are those that are leading towards a point of conclusion—the successive series draws a different link. For a series driven by an iconic protagonist, the events are linked by the ethos being challenged, even if they are challenged in different ways.

The discourse time of the *Raylene Pendle* novels is entirely devoted to Raylene's actions, indulging in several subplots besides the central investigation narrative. The moments of ellipsis once the story begins are comparatively short, and a good deal of Raylene's experience within the story world is dramatised. Deployed in first person, the narrative is entirely focused on what interests Pendle in her current predicaments. Spreading the discourse time across the range of subplots reveals a myriad of things that interest Raylene: her growing attraction to her client; the government conspiracy that blinded him; her dislike of her client's ghoulish assistant; her connections within the criminal fraternity comprised of hackers, thieves, and fences; her evolving friendships and connections; and the politics of various vampire houses. Many of these elements carry from the first novel to the second, which invites the reader to consider how the rich interests of Raylene's life continue outside of the discourse time rendered within the novels.

In contrast, Bear uses a far tighter field of focus for her discourse—because short stories and novellas are more compact than novels, and because the point of view is shared between multiple characters. This affords Bear the opportunity to foreground Sebastian's undead nature in a way that Priest's series cannot. When Sebastian speaks of feeling alone or bored due to his immortality (New Amsterdam, 63), the discourse reinforces his assertion through the events selected from the story time of the world and transformed into stories. While Pendle's point of view in the discourse time—and, subsequently, the assumption of things that are holding her interest—is spread across a breadth of subplots, Don Sebastian's is highly focused. His point of view guides the discourse time only when he is engaged in resolving a crime, or when he is trying to resolve the fundamental injustice he perceives as part-and-parcel of being an immortal who seeks diversion among his mortal compatriots.

Narratively, while Pendle has a broad field of interests that drive her eventual transformation, Don Sebastian 'comes alive' for a significantly smaller portion of the passage of time in the story world, and such moments are a temporary flare rather than the start of permanent change.

The use of point of view within the series also underscores the immortality of Sebastian very subtly through the use of a shared series protagonist. Sebastian is our sole point of view in the first story, but thereafter cedes the protagonists role to the character of Abigail Irene Garrett for the second, third, and forth instalments. He remains a central figure in these stories and returns as a point of view character as the series progresses past the fifth instalment. Garrett remains a strong presence in the later stories, but she ages and the final novella in the series begins with her death. Don Sebastian's point of view returns as the sole arbiter of the narrative discourse: the vampire is left alone, the last of his companions dead, and the reader is bereft of the other perspectives from earlier works. In this way, Bear uses the series itself to underpin the central themes of Sebastian's immortality and loneliness. Sebastian has outlived all the characters who connected the reader with the discourse, and while the series adopts a wider range of points of view over its life, ultimately Sebastian's point of view will reassert itself and be all that remains to the reader. Even as he forges new connections among the mortals of 1962, these point of view shifts suggest a cycle that always begins and ends with Sebastian's solitude, and implies any new connections will ultimately end the same way.

It is here that the use of series, rather than a single text, is significant: while Cherie Priest suggests her protagonists dramatic transformation are a potential aberration in *Hellbent*, the result of a crew coming together who are "damn near unique" (38), the discourse time is focused on Pendle's experiences with those mortals and the changes they invoke in both her internal and external status quo. The reader can accept they are a temporary departure from Pendle's habitual solitude, but very little of the discourse is devoted to the possibility. Pendle's reversion is, at best, a hypothetical possibility rather than a source of narrative focus. Instead, the reader's experience through the discourse time of the story is focused on the act of transformation—the isolation and boredom of undeath is a narrative problem to be solved, not a perpetual state. In contrast, the realities of Sebastian's undead immortality are laid out as part of the reader's narrative experience in *New Amsterdam*. To borrow a dictum often directed to writers, Bear uses the patterns established in earlier stories to show rather than tell. The loss of Abigail Irene Garrett is felt structurally within the discourse and becomes part of the reading experience as well as a narrative event.

Making the distinction between iconic and dramatic heroes, and how their stories interacted with progressive and successive series frameworks, quickly proved crucial to my process when writing series fiction. They allowed me to reflect on my prior series works and understand where they'd gone wrong, often drawing inspiration from iconic series heroes, but habitually writing them with distinct, stand-alone dramatic arcs with the expectation of series progression. Laws iconic hero not only provided the ability to identify two different types of series heroes. But also challenged some of the fundamental precepts of narrative structure that I have absorbed over a thirty-year career as both writer and writing mentor. The Dana Valkyrie novellas started with a clear intention: I would write a procedural hero whose adventures spread across five volumes, with the potential to iterate further stories in a successive series framework.

Making the decision proved to be easy, but crafting an iconic hero proved far more difficult than I imagined. While I have immersed myself in countless books and courses on planning stories and writing craft, my practice has often leant itself to more intuitive development than structured planning. To borrow a phrase from Becca Syme and Susan Bischoff, who interrogate the notion of intuitive practice in their popular writing guide, I do not habitually "show my work" regarding writing, although I can do so to "back up what our intuition is telling us, [and] to prove we can think 'the right way'" (67). While theories of narrative structure and intent are important to my understanding of craft, they are storytelling models I have internalised and submitted to, to borrow Delany's phrasing, or they are revision tools brought to bear after early drafts are completed or when discussing the work with others. When drafting the novellas for my creative project, it quickly became apparent an intuitive writing process was not serving me well. I habitual crafted with the dramatic arc in mind, building key scenes and conflicts to draw the reader forward. The drafts I produced were frequently unsatisfying, or repurposed Valkyrie as a dramatic hero to suit my established practice.

After several failed attempts to produce a viable draft, I decided on a two-pronged approach to mastering the rhythms of the iconic hero's story. First, informed by Delany's theory of internalising narrative models, I focused on reading texts featuring purely iconic heroes in prose form. Given the dominance of the dramatic narrative model, this meant seeking examples of the iconic hero in contemporary publishing such as Lee Child's *Jack Reacher* novels and stories, but also looking back to earlier periods where iconic heroes held more cache as a publishing strategy. While the dramatic hero has been the dominant form in contemporary publishing, Nick Mamatas' commentary on the shift from "the well tied bow" to the "ragged edge" ending in the short story market (61) inspired me to look back to a period which favoured the iconic, successive stories – the pulp era. For several months I devoted myself to reading series works by pulp authors, revisiting the detective stories of Raymond Chandler, Erle Stanley Gardner's *Sidney Zoom* stories, Robert E. Howard's *Conan the Barbarian* stories, *Solomon Kane* stories, and *Sailor Steve Costigan* boxing tales. These were supplemented by immersion in the works of other authors who favoured the iconic hero, such as Agatha Christie's *Poirot* novels and *Parker Pyne* stories, and modern antecedents such as Bear's *New Amsterdam* fantasy mysteries.

Concurrent with this reading was a dedicated attempt to use an alternative drafting process, rather than relying on my own intuition. Initially, I attempt to plan the stories using Laws' book on writing craft, *Beating the Story*, but ultimately found the process aligned itself too closely with my own instincts. Focusing on events naturally lent itself to building dramatic arcs, and I quickly abandoned the process. I used several other planning systems, among them Robert Ray's *The Weekend Novelist* and John Truby's *The Anatomy of Genre*, without success. Ultimately, the approach which finally helped me wrap my head around the iconic protagonists was found in Damon Suede's *Verbalize: Bringing Stories to Life and Life to Stories*. Suede's approach eschewed large-scale planning of plot elements and events in favour of a streamlined focus on a consistent undercurrent threading together a character's actions. These actions would be driven by a character's "void", or the unsolvable problem that drives their action (87). By aligning the actions taken with the unsolvable problem the character seeks to escape, it's possible to create an inner conflict that is depicted through action. While laid out as a popular writing guide, Suede builds on Constantin Stanislavski's principles of action, units, and objectives laid out in *The Actor Prepares*, adapting them for use in prose narrative. While Suede is nominally focused on dramatic action—Damon Suede is a nom-de-plume associated with his work as an author of queer romance—his process is born from years of writing for stage and screen. As Suede puts it, "scripts need to present their actors a healthy range of playable actions juicy and compelling enough to hold everyone's attention" (15), and his experiences has pushed him to focus on what characters do in a scene over their characteristics. Effectively, Suede echoes Stanislavski's argument that what happens on stage must be for a purpose (31), with a verb-driven objective (107). In Suede's view, "a character in a story is not a person, a profile, or an archetype, but an action figure, an entertaining device designed to perform a function within a story" (37), and narrative success relies upon the efficient and effective alignment of a character's actions across the narrative to showcase escalation and narrative progression (39). This focus on action is a natural fit for the procedural approach adopted by many iconic heroes, especially given their procedural focus, and I resolved to work to his method and approach the narrative in a different way. Here, I will address the usefulness of both these framings and how my understanding of Dana Valkyrie evolved through their usage.

My conception of Dana Valkyrie started with the internal void which drives the character, with a particular focus on a void I could explore across multiple iterations and contexts. For Suede, "your character's void becomes an unsolvable problem that drives all their actions" (87), representing a central pain, internal flaw, or dissatisfaction they grapple with in pursuing happiness. While this framing is common in writing guides, Suede's use of *unsolvable* proved significant. The implied promise of a dramatic narrative arc suggests the unsolvable problem will end in resolution over the course of the story, but when applied to iconic protagonists, it represents something different. Many iconic protagonists are driven by such voids, but their stories represent moments of short-term relief or distraction from the pain of their void. The challenges depicted in the discourse of the story are effectively salves for old wounds, not a healing of the wound itself.

The second pivotal aspect of Suede's method lies in use of transitive verbs to define a character. This framing typically occurs in two stages. The first involves selecting a transitive verb to represent the overarching, intentional action the character takes over the course of the story. This strategy emerges from and offers the hope of relief from their verb:

The action arises from their void and points them toward a happiness they believe/hope/pray might fill that inner emptiness permanently. However, and whoever they are, they pay attention in order to secure that happiness. The void creates the emotional context for all their decisions. (107)

This framing provides a useful method for seeing potential depth in procedural characters, as Suede suggests, "the void generates energy and the action expresses it in their world" (108). Here, he overtly echoes Stanislavski's belief that, "every objective must carry in itself the germ of action" (107), and it is in the action—rather than the noun—that the essence of drama can be found. Characters may be afflicted by internal conflict, but they are defined by the actions they take in order to alleviate that pain. Through repeated action, spread across multiple stories, a character could develop depths via the process of reader alignment and repeated action being brought into the field of significance.

Suede's methodology accompanies this central, strategic verb with a cloud of 20 to 30 tactical verbs, all drawn from synonyms of the strategic verb or synonyms of those synonyms; the author generates a series of aligned and meaningful actions stemming from the character's emotional core. Significantly, those verbs could then generate a crude outline for the book in which very few details were imagined in advance: the author could arrange the protagonist's tactical verbs in order, assigning the core action taken by the character in that scene in order. Rather than focusing on narrative, this structure focuses on the character's procedural steps, and transforms those verbs into a narrative by attaching short-term objectives as the story evolves. For example, I could know that at various stages of the novella Dana Valkyrie would enthuse, agitate, plague, strike, and fluster to solve problems within the narrative. Assembling these verbs allowed me to write to an alternate story framework, planning challenges that could provoke the actions rather than challenges that could provoke action and evolution across the story.

The challenge in building Dana Valkyrie now lay in finding the right verb and void, rather than the right story structure. My initial verbs focused on actions closely associated with the act of grappling or striking, taking my initial inspiration from Robert Howard's iconic pulp hero, the boxer Seve Costigan. In many ways, Costigan is the most one-note of the pulp heroes I encountered in my reading, and I was intrigued by the possibility of using series fiction to imbue depth into the hard-luck, trouble-in-every port character archetype and the significantly dated attitudes towards race and gender in Howard's work. While my initial fighting-based verbs provided some clarity, initial attempts to build Valkyrie around verbs such as strike, grasp, and counter did not imbue the character with the traits that resonated with me. It was not until I worked through two layers of synonyms associated with the above that I finally settled on the verb impress, from which everything could stem.

Once selected, the verb informed my choice of the character verb. Indeed, the relationship between the two is part of my dissatisfaction with my initial verb voices, as the character's void represents the moments where real complexity could emerge over the course of the series. Choosing impress prompted an important question: what drives a protagonist to impress others at all costs? The answer to this not only allowed me to see how Dana Valkyrie could iterate across multiple stories, but went on to inform the character's voice and status as an unreliable narrator. More importantly, a character focused on impressing others provides a rich seam of depth I draw into the field of significance for readers who engaged with two or more series texts. On the surface, Valkyrie's first-person narration is a tale spun for singular amusement, but through repetition of the same core motifs—coming ashore, getting into unexpected scrapes, fighting her way out by the skin of her teeth—the repetition of the moments Valkyrie choses to render in narration time take on new significance. She is not only motivated to impress those around her in the story, but those of us reading her tales; yet she herself is haunted by the prospect that she will never achieve the recognition and respect she believes she has forfeited with her lifestyle.

Dana Valkyrie remains a resolutely iconic hero within the faming of these stories. While there is a nominal reading order to these tales, they do not build or advance the character towards an epiphany. A reader may choose to engage with one, some, or all of the stories in the series, and remain confident their story experience will not be disrupted. However, I don't believe this choice sacrifices character complexity. Dana Valkyrie becomes, in effect, two different characters depending on the reader's exposure to, allegiance, and alignment with the character. While aspects of the character's complex interiority will come through in individual stories, repeated engagement across the texts in the series will add layers and depths through repeated exposure to that interiority, the commentary of the supporting characters around her, and the way the universe adjusts to her adventures. In the fifth volume—the first story written, and tentatively slated as a "series finale"—her adventures undergo a contextual shift with introducing the ongoing nemesis, crime boss Benython Gray, who will become a recurring background character in the subsequent novellas in the same way Valkyrie's mother appears as an ongoing element in the first five.

One advantage of drafting all five stories prior to release lay in developing elements in which an astute reader might find additional complexity. For example, surface level readings of a single text may reveal seeming anomalies in Dana's voice, where the semi-educated language she uses give way to more nuanced or eloquent takes. Such choices are intentional, in keeping with the framing of Dana as a character and narrator who seeks to impress. What strikes the singular reader as a momentary break in character can be read, across the length of the series, as evidence of Dana affecting elements of her speech in order to achieve specific effects, whether it's hiding her background and elocution from the crew whose esteem she values, impressing the Captain who employs her, or impressing the hypothetical reader who consumes these stories.

Similar nuance emerges through the stories repeated engagement with elements of Captain Rackham's past, the slow development of Big Wade from rookie to esteemed member of the crew, and the shifting relationships between Dana and key members of the crew, as well as secondary characters and antagonists who can emerge in later texts. Agent Fring, from *White Harbor War*, is earmarked to return in a future text, albeit one where he's engaged in a new scheme completely disconnected with the events of the first novella.

While I do not claim to have mastered series poetics, my engagement with issues of serial structures, temporality, and characterisation have provided me with the nuance and heightened awareness of how series texts worked that I craved at the beginning of my research. While informative to my own practice, I believe it's also a timely field of research in the changing interests of the publishing field. In my concluding chapter, I will briefly explore the growing prominence of series texts within the publishing field, and the broader issues violations of series norms represent. I believe this growing interest in series works may yet provide field for further studies of series poetics, and argue for case for a more nuanced discussion of seriality within the logic of the field.

GEORGE RR MARTIN IS NOT YOUR BITCH
A CONCLUSION

My central preoccupations throughout my research have been two-fold: to understand the poetics of series fiction well enough to tell better serialised stories; and to understand what makes a successful series on both the commercial and the artistic sides of the writer's craft. This desire led me on a journey that proved far more complex than I first imaged—in many respects, the logic of the field did not yet have a comprehensive method of articulating the myriad ways series fiction could be framed, let alone how it could achieve artistic effects.

In earlier chapters, I have argued the creation of series texts is often guided by the expectation of the market and the assumed logic of the field a writer can access. While writers cannot control or predict the reception of their work in the broader marketplace, both writers and publishers do make attempts to position their works within the broader field, and given the iterative creative development of series works these norms can often be in conversation with the field and the reading audience. As such, I believe an examination of how series can be received is a useful aspect of series poetics, especially in instances where agents have dramatically misjudged the broader assumptions around series work.

While they may not be able to articulate series norms, agents active within the publishing field clearly understand series poetics and moments when series norms have been violated. They can also sense and respond to the way series fiction draws seriality into the field of significance, and the way it informs the horizon of expectations with regards to subsequent texts.

At the time of writing, one of the most famous potential 'violations' of the horizon of expectations associated with series fiction is George RR Martins Song of Fire and Ice, which is famously unfinished and still in possession of a fanbase eager for a conclusion. In 2009, fantasy author Neil Gaiman wrote a blog post about entitlement issues with relation to series texts, inspired by a fan's questions about Martin's work habits.[1] At that time, Martin's best-selling Song of Fire and Ice series comprised four books in a progressive series that still had not reached an end-point, with a four-year gap since the release of the fourth book in 2005. A fan named Gareth had signed up for Martin's blog hoping for news about a new release, and then asked Gaiman a two-part question:

> 1. With blogs and twitter and other forms of social media do you think the audience has too much input when it comes to scrutinising the actions of an artist? If you had announced a new book two years ago and were yet to deliver do you think avoiding the topic on your blog would lead readers to believe you were being "slack"? By blogging about your work and life do you have more of a responsibility to deliver on your commitments?
>
> 2. When writing a series of books, like Martin is with "A Song of Ice and Fire" what responsibility does he have to finish the story? Is it unrealistic to think that by not writing the next chapter Martin is letting me down, even though if and when the book gets written is completely up to him? ("Entitlement Issues")

Gaiman answered both in the negative, summarising his

---

[1]. Gaiman would go on to repeat the phrase at a live performance of musical duo Paul and Storn's performance of parody song 'Write Like The Wind (George RR Martin)', and in live interviews.

response to the second question with a prefacing phrase: "George RR Martin is not your bitch" ("Entitlement Issues"). While the pithiness of this statement made it easy fodder for memes and pop-culture references, Gaiman's response delves further into the issue of entitlement and series texts. He notes that the complaint about Martin's process reads as though "buying the first book in a series was a contract with him," and emphasises such a contract does not exist: "You were paying ten dollars for the book you were reading, and I assume you enjoyed it because you want to know what happens next." ("Entitlement Issues") Central to Gaiman's point is the knowledge that authors are human, fallible, and prone to creative issues, with a focus on the book that exists rather than the books that might follow.

Gaiman's post continues to spark commentary on the internet, with Brent Weeks arguing that the implied promise of "Book 1" includes a reasonable right to seeing the series finished. He suggests that while readers have no legal right to a finished series, writers have an obligation and failing to meet those obligations results in detrimental effects in the market for mid-list authors whose potential readership is gun-shy about starting an unfinished series (Weeks). Gaiman is similarly referenced in the title of Shayne Ryan's 2017 essay for *Paste* magazine. Ryan agrees that readers are not owed a final book. However, he also argues that the commercial relationship established by years of purchasing and discussing Martin's work suggests that readers should receive yearly updates about the next book's progress (Ryan). While both essays accept the central premise of Gaiman's argument, both take issue with the way Martin violates the norms around the release and completion of series texts. This suggest that readers can be sensitive to, and vocal about, violations of those norms.

While Martin is currently the highest profile example of these violations in the fantasy fiction space, similar discussions have emerged around the works of Patrick Rothfuss and other fantasy authors whose series have remained unfinished, whether it is because of writerly speed, the author's death, or a lack of interest by their publisher. Notably, these examples are progressive series whose release schedule has moved away from the once-a-year norms established within the publishing industry. The sense of entitlement Gaiman and those arguing with him speak of are predicated on those norms, contrasted against the norms of the progressive series and the anxiety around an end-point that might never be reached. Legally, the author owes the reader nothing but the book being read, but the social contract seems to be another matter entirely. Gaiman's solution—to treat each book as its own entity, disconnected from the rest of the series—doesn't seem to satisfy readers who do not wish to be suspended in the ellipsis between series instalments, and would rather have the series progression reach its conclusion.

The question of what writers owe their audiences is not limited to series texts, and the contract is a recurring metaphor in writing advice. Melbourne-based editor Liam Peiper advises writers that "to write is to make a contract with a future reader to enlighten, or at least entertain," (Peiper), while Ann Aguirre uses the same metaphor to describe the unspoken promises that narratives make in her Writer Unboxed article, *Contract Between Writer and Reader*. The horizon of expectations may begin before the text is opened, but it is refined and redirected in these opening moments and throughout the text. In a progressive series, this often pulls the eventual end-point of the series itself into the field of significance for the reader, and sets expectations accordingly. George RR Martin may not be the reader's bitch, but nor has he fulfilled the narrative expectations and norms associated with the form he has selected. Each instalment of *A Song of Fire and Ice* may be satisfying as a novel, but they are not finished in the way a stand-alone text is when the denouement is reached. As a series, the field of significance has shifted to incorporate an ongoing continuity and causality between individual texts. While each book possesses a narrative climax, the expectations set by the progressive series is that these climaxes are subservient to an ultimate endpoint at the series conclusion, and to read out of sequence or to leave the text unfinished is effectively reading in bad faith.

Conversely, an unfinished progressive series violates the expected chain of causality that has become common in fiction—the chain of cause and effect has not achieved its ultimate expression. When *A Game of Thrones* concludes with the execution of Ned Stark and the scattering of his family, both narrative expectation and series convention suggest that things are just beginning. Through narrative and meta-textual queues, each instalment of *A Song of Fire and Ice* pulls the final resolution of who will sit on the Iron Throne into the field of significance as the series end-point, and Stark's death represents an important moment of transition that re-contextualises our expectations, but is not a final resolution. We may have reached the end of Ned Stark's involvement in the story, and his role as a framing device through which events are filtered, but his death does not satisfy as an overall resolution of the story.

Despite Gaiman's assertions, the progressive model links the current text to the ultimate endpoint, and its value as a narrative artifact is predicated upon the inbuilt relationship with the other texts. While individual texts may hold other values, to read them out of order or leave the series unfinished is to read counter to the aspects of narrative the text pulls into the field of significance through its continuity, ongoing character development, and cues embedded in textual metadata. Martin's unfinished series violates commercial norms, established by the broader market conditions and the narrative itself. While the purchase of the first book may not constitute a contract promising a final resolution, the violation of these norms remains a contentious point amid the interpretive community in which Martin's works are read.

Questions of series norms were a relatively minor issue within the field of traditional publishing, where long-running series were comparatively rare, and those series which existed frequently resolved at the end of a trilogy. However, the inability to clearly identify or understand those norms felt central to many of the issues I'd faced when trying to write series fiction in the past. Understanding both scholarly and practice led research allows for a clearer articulation of the logic of the field around series works, and allows for a clearer communication about series goals, techniques, and pitfalls. This research feels particularly timely, as series works have been receiving increased attention in many parts of speculative fiction field. Two major speculative fiction awards have added "Best Series" categories in recent years. The first of these debuted in 2015, when the Australian-based Aurealis Awards launched the Sara Douglas Book Series award as an ongoing category in 2015, seeking to recognise fiction series "whose whole are greater than the sum of their parts" (Tehani). Two years later, the Hugo Awards hosted by the annual WorldCon science fiction convention added the Best Series as a recurring category alongside awards celebrating the best works of science fiction and fantasy at novel, novella, novelette, and short story released in a twelve-month period.

Held yearly at the annual World Science Fiction Convention, the Hugos are voted on by the attending and associate members of the current, and previous, convention. While Hugo shortlists have often been contentious, with the "Sad Puppies" movement of recent years showcasing the procedure's vulnerability to internet-based nomination campaigns, they also represent a source of recognition and symbolic value within the genre. The inaugural Best Series award featured a short-list of six fictional series, with the prize eventually going to Lois McMaster Bujold for the 23-novels in her science-fiction-based *Vorkosigan Saga*. Bujold would take the category in 2018 with her World of the Five Gods fantasy, a seven-book series whose first volume was published in in 2001 and its seventh published in 2017 ("Hugo Winners").

Although the symbolic capital generated by an Aurealis Award may be smaller than the Hugos, courtesy of its national focus, the awards are reported on in industry publications such as Locus Magazine and the File440 blog, and being shortlisted for the awards can draw attention from international publishers and agents. My interest here lies not in how much capital these awards can generate, but in the series formats they seek to celebrate. In order to manage submissions, both awards create a taxonomy of series and guidelines for eligibility. For the Hugos, works eligible to win the best series must be:

> *A multi-volume science fiction of fantasy story, unified by elements such as plot, character, setting, and presentation appearing in at least three (3) volumes consisting in total of at least 240,000 words by the close of the previous calendar year, at*

least one volume of which was published in the previous calendar year. ("2017 Hugo Awards")

This guideline is further clarified by three sections of the WSFS Constitution, the governing body behind the awards. The first of these touches of issues of temporality regarding series works—while it is relatively easy to determine when a new novel or short story is eligible for each year's awards, long-running series have the potential to dominate. It is worth noting here, as a contrast, the framing of series eligibility in the Aurealis Awards.

> **3.3.5.1:** *Previous losing finalists in the Best Series category shall be eligible only upon the publication of at least two (2) additional installments consisting in total of at least 240,000 words after they qualified for their last appearance on the final ballot and by the close of the previous calendar year.*
>
> **3.8.3:** *If any series and a subset series thereof both receive sufficient nominations to appear on the final ballot, only the version which received more nominations shall appear.*
>
> **3.8.6:** *If there are more than two works in the same category that are episodes of the same dramatic presentation series or that are written works that have an author for single author works, or two or more authors for co-authored works, in common, only the two works in each category that have the most nominations shall appear on the final ballot. ("Best Series")*

While the focus is multiple volumes, the awards also include guidelines for dealing with hierarchies within a series, covering situations where a series may have an overarching brand and sub-set series within it. In this respect, they open themselves up to the three branches of series fiction identified by Watson—Progressive, Successive, and Format—but also foreground narrative linkage as a stronger connector than format or setting.

Once again, the criteria associated with the awards reads like an attempt to define series fiction—or, at least, the series fiction whose symbolic value the award will recognise within their respective fields. What is intriguing about the Aurealis award is not that its definition differs from the taxonomy at work in the Hugo category, but that the taxonomy at work is weighted toward a specific approach to series fiction. According to the initial press release, The Sara Douglas Book Series Awards—named for the flagship author of HarperVoyager's Australian fantasy line— seeks to recognise that "there are book series that are greater as a whole than the sum of their parts." In laying out explicit requirements, this approach is further refined with the statement that:

> *For the purpose of the Sara Douglass Book Series Award, a "series" is defined as a continuing ongoing story told through two or more books, which must be considered as ending in one of the years covered by the judging period. (Tehani)*

The inclusion of finished is telling here, both for its recognition that there are different series models, and for the preference given to progressive, rather than successive, series model. While these guidelines serve a practical purpose—the Aurealis Awards are judged by a small panel of volunteers, rather than drawing from a wide voting pool of readers who nominate works they are already familiar with—these awards bestow symbolic capital upon works included in both the shortlists and the finalists. They become, in effect a marker for what "quality" series fiction may be, and imply the progression towards a narrative end point as a central requirement. While categories such as best novel and best short story obligate judges to read all the works released within the current year, introducing a series category does not mount the potential workload on judges in quite the same way. After all, books released within a calendar year presents a finite date range and number of texts. Series fiction may include texts published years, or decades, prior to the year of the award, and may require engagement with dozens of texts of varying lengths.

This stricture serves to reinforce a vision of the series that lies in keeping with fantasy fiction's tendency towards the trilogy and keeps the award process manageable for a small judging team who produce the Aurealis shortlists and winners. However,

I cannot help but think of the series fictions this would exclude when applied to other genres. It is a vision of the series that proves a poor fit for many of the series works I've studied. It is also a description that would exclude several series texts within the fantasy genre: Robert Howard's *Conan* stories, for example, and their more contemporary antecedents, such as Garth Nix *Sir Fitz and Mr Hereward* stories. While these series may reach an ending, under the commercial aspect of the rules when collected together or no longer published, they do not fit the demand for series that tells a progressing story across the length. Each text is intended as a stand-alone narrative, albeit one that shares a world and thematic resonances with other series stories.

The focus on the progressive narrative in the Aurealis Award guidelines provides an intriguing point of differentiation between the two award categories, especially in light of the short-lists that have been established for both awards in their short existence. The Aurealis Awards call for series that tells a story also pulls into focus one of the key differentiating points between the progressive and successive series modes, inviting us to consider what the story means within the series context, and in particular how it may differ from a character whose narratives are "loosely connected" (Tehani). Looking back at my own experiences writing series, a focus on clear character arcs and endpoints proved a detriment to creative process, and stood at odds with the genre I hoped to allude to in my work. As my research has shown, this is not the only structural approach to series characters, nor is it the only way to adequately explore the interiority of a character or achieve narrative effects.

In this book, I have laid out my motivations and goals in pursuing an understanding of series fiction. Initially, I wished only to ease my discomfort with series formats, exorcising the ghosts of prior projects that never hit the creative goals I set for myself. I hoped to understand where I had gone wrong and write a "successful" series that pleased both my own creative ambitions and the broader market. As I studied the series format in depth, my goals became more complex. Despite its growing popularity in both backlist-driven and velocity-driven publishing models, the field's broader understanding of how series fiction achieves its artistic effects and the craft considerations implicit in their creation are woefully under-articulated. Even the pivotal insights found in the works Robin Laws, Jason Mittell, and Victor Watson are inaccessible to emerging writers grappling with series structures, as the three are better known in the fields of game design (Laws) and academia (Mittell, Watson). Yet, they each identify an aspect of seriality that holds productive power for a writer, whether it is the approach to characterisation, the acknowledgement of time's role in the reading process, or the unifying structural model that governs the series. While it is tempting to consider these three aspects in binary terms—series works may be dramatic or iconic, or progressive or successive, and follow myriad release schedules—a more productive use of these theories is to consider them a spectrum from which the story draws its norms and regime of verisimilitude.

I do not present this research with the assumption that the task of charting series poetics is completed, nor that the tools it adds to the logic of the field are of use to all agents active within the publishing field. To return to John B. Thompson's metaphor of grammar, this books represents the series conventions and rules of most use to my process, in the analysis of published series which informed my process, and those authors who I most often speak to about serial works. The ultimate success of my interrogation lies in the reception of the creative works generated —those included in this thesis, and thee novellas not included in this this document—but also on the ability to leverage series poetics when a reader is familiar with only part of the overall series.

Writers have—and will continue to—write series fiction without developing a nuanced or conscious understanding of the conventions and norms they engage with. One doesn't need to understand the rules of grammar to use it intuitively, but there is power in moving beyond intuition. Articulating series norms allows a greater application of craft in the writing process, from the creation of early drafts through to the revision and refinement of the creative text. An awareness of the market's expectations gives writers and other agents within the publishing field something to work to, or work against, when striving towards commercial and artistic success, and the ability to see how past successes have invoked or drawn seriality as a significant element of the text. In a world where series fiction is rapidly growing more prominent, simultaneously providing more opportunities to write successful series fiction while challenging long-established industry norms, an evolving and nuanced understanding of series poetics is a powerful addition to the logic of the field for writers, publishers, and readers alike.

BIBLIOGRAPHY

"2017 Hugo Awards." *The Hugo Awards*, www.thehugoawards.org/hugo-history/2017-hugo-awards/. Accessed 6 Jun 2018.

Aaron, Rachel. "How I Went From Writing 2,000 Words A Day to 10,000 Words A Day." *Pretentious Title*, 8 June 2011, thisblogisaploy.blogspot.com/2011/06/how-i-went-from-writing-2000-words-day.html. Accessed 12 Dec 2023.

Aguirre, Ann. "Contract Between Writer and Reader." *Writer Unboxed*, 14 Mar 2012, https://writerunboxed.com/2012/03/14/contract-between-writer-and-reader/. Accessed 12 Dec 2023.

Alter, Alexander. "Fast-Paced Best Seller: Author Russell Blake Thrives on Volumes." The *Wall Street Journal*, 7 Jan 2014, www.wsj.com/articles/SB10001424052702303640604579298604044404682. Accessed 12 Dec 2023.

Altman, Rick. *The American Film Musical / Rick Altman*. Indiana University Press, 1987.

Anderton, Joanne. *2014 Snapshot Archive: Joanne Anderton*. Blog, 8 June 2016, austsfsnapshot.wordpress.com/2016/06/08/2014-snapshot-archive-joanne-anderton/. Accessed 12 Dec 2023.

Anderson, Kevin J. Interview with Joanna Penn. "23 Million Books Sold. How To Have A Successful Long Term Writing Career With Kevin J Anderson". *The Creative Penn*, 17 October 2016, www.thecreativepenn.com/2016/10/17/23-million-books-kevin-j-anderson/. Accessed 14 Dec 2022.

Ball, Peter M. *Horn*. Twelfth Planet Press, 2009.

---. *Bleed*. Twelfth Planet Press, 2010.

Bear, Elizabeth. *Ad Eternum*. Subterranean, 2012.

---. *New Amsterdam*. Diamond Comic Distributors, 2008.

---. *Seven for a Secret*. Subterranean, 2009.

---. *The White City*. Subterranean Press, 2010

Bell, James Scott. *Plot & Structure: Techniques and Exercises for Crafting a Plot That Grips Readers From Start To Finish*. Writers Digest Books, 2004.

---. *How To Write Short Stories and Use Them To Further Your Writing Career*. eBook, Compendium Press, 2016.

"Best Series" *The Constitution of the World Science Fiction Society, as of August 22, 2017*, www.wsfs.org/rules-of-the-world-science-fiction-society/archive-of-wsfs-rules/rules-of-the-world-science-fiction-society/archive-of-wsfs-rules/wsfs-rules-as-of-worldcon-75-2017/, PDF File. Accessed 12 Dec 2023.

Bordwell, David. *Poetics of Cinema*. 1st ed., Routledge, 2007, doi:10.4324/9780203941898.

Bourdieu, Pierre. Translated by Randal Johnson. *The Field of Cultural Production: Essays on Art and Literature*. Columbia University Press, 1993.

Bosman, Julie. "Impatience Has Its Reward: Books Are Rolled Out Faster." *The New York Times*, 10 Feb. 2014, www.nytimes.-

com/2014/02/11/books/impatience-has-its-reward-books-are-rolled-out-faster.html. Accessed 11 November 2023.

Buckell, Tobias S. "How I Used Kickstarter To Reboot A Book Series." TobiasBuckell.com, 17 Mar 2012, tobiasbuckell.com/how-i-used-kickstarter-to-reboot-a-book-series/. Accessed 12 December 2023

"Bleed Review" *ScaryMinds - Horror's Last Colonial Outpost*, 2011, www.scaryminds.com/reviews/2011/book87.php. Accessed 2 January 2020.

Campbell, Joseph. *The Hero with a Thousand Faces*. 3rd ed, New World Library, 2008.

Chandler, Raymond. "Finger Man". *Collected Stories*. Everyman's Library, 2002, pp. 105-163.

---. "Goldfish". *Collected Stories*. Everyman's Library, 2002, pp. 473-521.

Child, Lee. *Tripwire*. eBook, Transworld Digital, 2008.

---. *The Visitor*. eBook, Transworld Digital, 2008

"Creative Writing PhD Thesis Format." University of Queensland website, my.uq.edu.au/information-and-services/higher-degree-research/my-thesis/1-thesis-preparation/creative-writing-phd-thesis-format. Accessed 12 December 2023.

Cron, Lisa. *Story Genius: How To Use Brain Science To Go Beyond Outlining And Write A Riveting Novel*. Ten Speed Press, 2016

Culler, Jonathan. *Structuralist Poetics*. Rutledge Classics, 1975.

Daniels, Beth. *Beginners Guide To Story Arcs for Trilogies and Series With A Bow to Spin-offs And Sequels*. 3 Media Press, 2017.

Dane, Lauren. *Coming Undone*. eBook, Penguin, 2010.

---. *Laid Bare*. eBook, Penguin, 2009.

Delany, Samuel R. *About Writing: Seven Essays, Four Letters, and Five Interviews*. Wesleyan University Press, 2005.

Denson, Shane. "To be continued...«: Seriality and Serialization in Interdisciplinary Perspective." *Proceedings of: What Happens Next: The Mechanics of Serialization. Graduate Conference at the University of Amsterdam, March 25–26, 2011. In: JLTonline. 17.06.2011, www.jltonline.de/index.php/conferences/article/view/346/1004*. Accessed 12 Dec, 2023.

Derrida, Jacques. "The Law of Genre." Translated by Avital Ronell *Critical Inquiry*, vol. 7, no. 1, 1980, pp. 55–81, doi.org/10.1086/448088.

Forster, E. M. *Aspects of the Novel*. Penguin, 1962.

Fox, Chris. *5,000 Words Per Hour: Write Faster, Write Smarter*. eBook, Chris Fox Writes, 2015.

Fugate, Francis L. and Roberta B. Fugate. *Secrets of the Worlds Best Selling Writer: The Story-Telling Techniques of Erle Stanley Gardner*. eBook, Graymalkin Media, 1980

Gaiman, Neil. "The Pornography of Genre, or the Genre of Pornography." *Journal of the Fantastic in the Arts*, vol. 24, no. 3, 2014, pp. 399–407.

---. "Entitlement Issues." *Neil Gaiman's Journal*, 12 May 2009, journal.neilgaiman.com/2009/05/entitlement-issues.html. Accessed 12 Dec 2023.

Gracie, Anne. *Bride By Mistake*. eBook, Penguin eBooks, 2012.

Grady, Constance. "Meet a New Kind of Book, Designed for the Age of Peak TV." *Vox*, 6 Aug. 2018, www.vox.com/culture/2018/8/6/16849756/serial-box-serialized-books-peak-tv. Accessed 4 Jan. 2020.

Gruber, Frank. *The Pulp Jungle*. Sherborne Press, 1967,

Hendrix, Grady. *The Great Stephen King Reread: The Green Mile*. Tor.com, 19 June 2015, www.tor.com/2015/06/19/the-great-stephen-king-reread-the-green-mile/. Accessed 2 Jan. 2020.

Howard, *Robert E. The Sailor Steve Costigan Series and Other Boxing Tales*. eBook, e-artnow, 2016.

"Hugo Award Winners By Category" Science Fiction Awards Database, www.sfadb.com/Hugo_Awards_Winners_By_Category#null. Accessed 12 Dec 2023.

Huston, Charlie. *A Dangerous Man*. Ballantine, 2006.

Jauss, David. "Stacking Stones: Building a Unified Short Story Collection". *Alone With All That Could Happen: Rethinking Conventional Wisdom About The Craft Of Fiction Writing*. F+W Publications, 2008, pp 149-183.

Jauss, Hans Robert. *Toward an Aesthetic of Reception / Hans Robert Jauss*. Brighton : Harvester Press, 1982.

Keyes, J. Gregory. "Wakes The Narrow Forest." *Dragon Magazine #249*, 2 July 1998, pp 58-65.

Keyes, Greg. *The Hounds of Ash and Other Tales of Fool Wolf*. Edge Science Fiction & Fantasy Publishing, 2008.

Laquintano, Timothy. *Mass Authorship and the Rise of Self-Publishing*. University Of Iowa Press, 2016.

Law, Graham. *Serializing Fiction in the Victorian Press*. Palgrave Macmillan UK, 2000, doi:10.1057/9780230286740.

Laws, Robin. *Beating The Story: How To Understand, Map, and Elevate Every Story*. eBook, Gameplaywright, 2017.

---. "Introduction." *The New Hero*, edited by Robin Laws. Stone Skin Press, 2012.

"List of Forgotten Realms Novels." *Wikipedia, The Free Encyclopedia*, Wikimedia Foundation, en.wikipedia.org/wiki/List_of_Forgotten_Realms_novels. Accessed 12 Dec 2023

McGuire, Seanan. *Rosemary and Rue*. Daw Books, 2009.

McGurl, Mark. *Everything and Less : the Novel in the Age of Amazon*. Verso, 2021.

Mamatas, Nick. "How to End A Story" *Starve Better: Surviving The Endless Horrors Of The Writing Life*. Apex Publications, 2011, pp. 57-64.

Martin, George R. R. *A Game of Thrones: Books 1-5* (Omnibus). eBook, HarperCollins, 2012.

Mittell, Jason. *Complex TV : The Poetics of Contemporary Television Storytelling*. New York University Press, 2015.

Mod, Craig. "Subcompact Publishing: Simple Tools And Systems For Digital Publishing". *CriagMod.com*, Nov 2012, craigmod.com/journal/subcompact_publishing/. Accessed 12 Dec 2023

Newman, Kim. "Egyptian Avenue." *The Mammoth Book of Best New Horror 14*, edited by Stephen Jones. Robinson, 2003, pp. 330-345.

---. *Mysteries of the Diogenes Club*. MonkeyBrain Books, 2010.

---. *The Man from the Diogenes Club*. MonkeyBrain Books, 2006.

---. *The Secret Files of the Diogenes Club*. Monkeybrain Books, 2007.

Nimmo, Maureen. "Tracing Adult Fiction Series." *Technicalities*, vol. 19, no. 10, 1999, p. 4.

Palmquist, Susan. *Writing The Continuing Series And Trilogy.* Coldstream Publishing, 2016.

Pavel, Thomas. "Literary Genres as Norms and Good Habits." *New Literary History*, vol. 34, no. 2, 2003, p. 201.

Peiper, Liam. "Writing Is A Contract With A Reader." *Writers Victoria*, 6 February 2016, writersvictoria.org.au/resources/writing-tips-and-tools/writing-contract-the-reader. Accessed 15 June 2018.

Penn, Joanna. "Writing A Series: 7 Continuation Issues To Avoid." *The Creative Penn*, 2 Nov. 2011, www.thecreativepenn.com/2011/11/02/writing-a-series-continuation-issues/. Accessed 3 January 2020.

Platt, Sean, and Johnny B. Truant. *Iterate and Optimize.* eBook, Sterling & Stone, 2016.

---. *Write. Publish. Repeat: The No-Luck-Required Guide To Self-Publishing Success.* Sterling & Stone, 2013.

Priest, Cherie. *Bloodshot.* eBook, Titan Books, 2011.

---. *Bloodshot.* eBook, Titan Books, 2011.

---. "Is the Cheshire Red Reports Series Going..". *Goodreads: Cherie Priest Q&A.* www.goodreads.com/questions/90305-is-the-cheshire-red-reports-series-going. Accessed 2 Jan. 2020.

Quinn, Kenneth. *How Literature Works : the Nature of the Literary Experience.* Australian Broadcasting Commission, 1982.

Rawlinson, Kevin. "Jack Reacher Series Author 'Quits and Lets His Brother Step In'." *The Guardian*, 18 January 2020, www.theguardian.com/books/2020/jan/18/jack-reacher-series-author-lee-child-quits-and-lets-brother-step-in. Accessed 12 Dec 2023.

Reid, Calvin. "Startup Serial Box Wants To Be the 'HBO for Readers.'" *PublishersWeekly.Com*, 18 September 2015, www.publishersweekly.com/pw/by-topic/digital/content-and-e-books/article/68116-startup-serial-box-wants-to-be-the-hbo-for-readers.html. Accessed 20 January 2020.

Rusch, Kristine Katherine/ "The Business Rusch: Advertising, Print Editions, And Traditional Publishing (Discoverability Part One)." *KrisWrites.com*, 20 Nov 2013, kriswrites.com/2013/11/20/the-business-rusch-advertising-print-editions-and-traditional-publishing-discoverability-part-one/. Accessed 4 Jan 2023.

Ryan, Marie-Laure. *A New Anatomy of Storyworlds : What Is, What If, As If,* Ohio State University Press, 2022. *ProQuest Ebook Central*, http://ebookcentral.proquest.com/lib/uql/detail.action?docID=7045425.

Created from uql on 2024-05-24 23:19:04.

Ryan, Marie-Laure and Thon, Jan-Noël. "Introduction. *Storyworlds across Media: Toward a Media-Conscious Narratology.* University of Nebraska Press, 2014. *Project MUSE* muse.jhu.edu/book/31010.

Ryan, Shane. "George R.R. Martin Is Not Our Bitch, But the Dude Could Throw Us a Damn Bone". *Paste Magazine*, 3 Jan 2017, www.pastemagazine.com/books/game-of-thrones/george-rr-martin-is-not-our-bitch-but-the-dude-cou. Accessed 12 June 2023.

Salesses, Matthew. *Craft In The Real World: Rethinking Fiction Writing And The Workshop.* eBook, Catapult, 2021

Salvatore, R. A. *Streams of Silver.* Wizards of the Coast, 2009.

Smith, Dean Wesley. "A Second Way To Go." *DeanWesleySmith.com*, 9 May 2023, deanwesleysmith.com/a-second-way-to-go/. Accessed 12 May 2023.

Smith, Murray. *Engaging Characters: Fiction, Emotion and the Cinema*. Oxford University Press, 1995.

Snyder, Blake. *Save The Cat: The Last Book On Screenwriting You'll Ever Need*. eBook, Michael Weise Productions, 2005.

Stanislavksi, Constantin. Translated by Elizabeth Reynolds Hapgood. *An Actor Prepares*. Bloomsbury Publishing, 2013.

Stross, Charlie. "Introducing Dead Lies Dreaming." *Antipope.org*, 31 Dec 2019, www.antipope.org/charlie/blog-static/2019/12/introducing-dead-lies-dreaming.html. Accessed 8 January 2023.

Suede, Damon. *Verbalize: Bring Stories To Life And Life To Stories*. Evil Mastermind, 2017.

Syme, Becca, and Susan Bischoff. *Dear Writer, Are You Intuitive?* Hummingbird Books, 2022.

Tan, Charles. "Bibliophile Stalker: Book Review: Bleed by Peter M. Ball." *Bibliophile Stalker*, 29 Nov. 2010, charles-tan.blogspot.com/2010/11/book-review-bleed-by-peter-m-ball.html. Accessed 2 Jan. 2020.

Tehani. "Sara Douglass Book Series Awards Open to Entries." *Aurealis Awards*, 26 May 2018, aurealisawards.org/2018/05/27/sara-douglass-book-series-awards-open-to-entries/.

Thompson, John. B. *Merchants of Culture: The Publishing Business In The Twenty-First Century*. 2nd ed. Penguin, 2012.

"Title: Soho Golem." The Internet Speculative Fiction Database, 13 Oct. 2004, www.isfdb.org/cgi-bin/title.cgi?349381. Accessed 12 Dec 2023.

Todorov, Tzvetan. *The Fantastic: A Structural Approach to a Literary Genre*. Translated by Richard Howard, Press of Case Western Reserve University, 1973.

Truby, John. *The Anatomy of Story: 22 Steps To Becoming A Master Storyteller*. Picador, 2007

Vogler, Christopher. *The Writer's Journey: Mythic Structure for Storytellers and Screenwriters*. 2nd rev. ed, Pan, 1999.

Vermeule, Blakey. *Why Do We Care About Literary Characters?* Johns Hopkins University Press, 2010.

Watson, Victor. *Reading Series Fiction: From Arthur Ransome to Gene Kemp*. Taylor and Francis, 2000.

---. "41. Series Fiction (Part II: Forms and genres)." *International Companion Encyclopaedia of Children's Literature*, edited by Peter Hunt. Routledge, Taylor & Francis Group, 2004.

Weeks, Brent. "Revisiting "George Rr Martin Is Not Your Bitch." *SciFiNow*, 10 Nov 2011, www.scifinow.co.uk/blog/brent-weeks-opinion-column-george-rr-martin-is-not-your-bitch/. Accessed 12 Dec 2023.

"What's With the Name '20BooksTo50K'?" *20Booksto50K Facebook Group Guide*, 6 January 2020, www.facebook.com/groups/20Booksto50k/learning_content/?filter=598375874282415&post=836113530181118. Accessed 12 December 2023.

Whitehead, Adam. "The Wertzone: Melanie Rawn's SPELLBINDER Series Cancelled." *The Wertzone*, 30 Sept. 2010, thewertzone.blogspot.com/2010/09/melanie-rawns-spellbinder-series.html.

Wiesnar, Karen S. *Writing the Fiction Series: The Complete Guide for Novels and Novellas*. eBook. Writers's Digest Books, 2013.

Wilkins, Kim. and Lisa Bennett. *Writing Bestsellers: Love, Money, and Creative Practice*. Cambridge University,

Wilkins, Kim. "Do The Hustle: Writing In A Post-Digital Publishing World." *Sydney Review of Books*, 27 September 2019, sydneyreviewofbooks.com/essay/do-the-hustlewriting-in-a-post-digitalpublishing-world/. Accessed 12 December 2023.

---. "The Process of Genre: Authors, Readers, Institutions." *TEXT: Journal of Writing and Writing Courses*, vol. 9, no. 2, 2005. Accessed 12 Dec 2023.

ABOUT THE AUTHOR

DR. PETER M. BALL is an author, publisher, and RPG gamer whose love of speculative fiction emerged after exposure to *The Hobbit*, *Star Wars*, David Lynch's *Dune*, and far too many games of *Dungeons and Dragons* before the age of 7. He's spent the bulk of his life working as a creative writing tutor, with brief stints as a performance poet, gaming convention organizer, online content developer, non-  profit arts manager, GenreCon convener, and d20 RPG publisher. He holds a PhD in writing from the University of Queensland.

He's the author of the Miriam Aster series and the Keith Murphy Urban Fantasy Thrillers, three short story collections, and more stories, articles, poems, and RPG material than he'd care to count. He's the brain-in-charge at Brain Jar Press, publishes his own work through the GenrePunk Books imprint, and resides in Brisbane, Australia, with his partner and two cats.

Peter can be found online at:
www.petermball.com

- facebook.com/Petermball
- instagram.com/petermball
- bsky.app/profile/petermball.bsky.social
- threads.net/@petermball

GENREPUNK NINJA
A NEWSLETTER ABOUT WRITING & PUBLISHING

Are you a fiction writer, indie, or small press publisher ready to level up your business? Are *you* interested in hearing Peter M. Ball's thoughts on writing and publishing? GenrePunk Ninja is for you!

Sign up for Peter's writing and publishing newsletter to get his perspectives on the craft and business of writing delivered directly to your inbox.

FIND OUT MORE AT HTTP://GENREPUNK.NINJA

www.ingramcontent.com/pod-product-compliance
Lightning Source LLC
Chambersburg PA
CBHW030306100526
44590CB00012B/535